From The Kitchen Table To The Conference Table

Family Business Communication

Laura Michaud

Copyright © 2004, Laura Michaud
For questions regarding
*From the Kitchen Table
to The Conference Table:
Family Business Communication*
e-mail: Laura@FamilyBusinessSuccess.net
Office: 630-835-0333
Fax: 630-833-4478

All rights reserved. No part of this book may be reproduced or transmitted in any form or by any means, electronic or mechanical, including photocopying, recording, retrieval system, without written permission from the author, except for the inclusion of brief quotations in a review.

03 04 05 06 HH 10 9 8 7 6 5 4 3 2 1
Printed in the United States of America
ISBN: 0-9744149-4-8
Library of Congress Control #: 2003115772
Printed in the United States of America

Requests for permission to make copies of any part of this work can be made to:

PO Box 8006
Hilton Head Island, SC 29938
1-866-372-2636
info@cameopublications.com
www.cameopublications.com

BUS007000
Business & Economics / Business Communication / General
BUS060000 Business & Economics / Small Business

Cover designed by
David Josephson
Cameo Publications, LLC

About Laura Michaud, MBA

Laura Michaud believes in people and in results, and her track record proves it. As a third-generation owner of Beltone Electronics, she was instrumental in growing sales by over 300% in less than two decades by focusing on sales, marketing, and most of all, people. Internally, she focused on employee communications and morale, resulting in the lowest turnover rate in the history of Beltone; externally, she launched the first nationwide customer assurance program, which led to substantial market share growth.

Before selling Beltone in 1997, she led the company's sales department to grossing over $150 million in revenue. Today, as owner of The Michaud Group, Laura shares her expertise by working with family-business organizations and their employees to help them improve their performance, enhance their relationships, and work through the various transitions that are inherent in family-owned companies. As a previous owner of Beltone, Executive VP of Sales and Marketing, and a board of director member, Laura is a family business expert who intimately understands the challenges facing today's family businesses.

Laura brings a dynamic presentation style and a wealth of credibility to her coaching, consulting, writing, and presentations. She is one of today's most sought-after experts in family business, Laura has been interviewed by or her articles have appeared in such media outlets as *Entrepreneur*, *Executive Excellence*, *Family Business*, and many others. Her areas of specialization include succession planning, building relationships between non-family and family employees, creating organizational structure, board development, increasing the bottom line through better employee and customer management, lowering employee attrition, creating a work/life balance, and increasing referrals and repeat business.

Laura earned her MBA from Loyola University. She is a member of Family Firm Institute and the National Speakers Association.

Dedication

This book is dedicated to all family businesses, large and small, who long for family peace, continuity, and success. May you gain the insights to create the work and life of your dreams.

Table of Contents

About the Author 3
Acknowledgements 9
Introduction 11
Chapter One:
   The Good, the Bad, and the Ugly of
   Working with the Ones You Love .. 15
Chapter Two:
   Family Meetings ~
   *The First Step to Improving
   Family and Business Relations*....... 33
Chapter Three:
   From Business Savvy
   to People Savvy ~
   *How Communication and Behavioral
   Styles Affect Business Success* 55
Chapter Four:
   Understanding You ~
   What it all Means............................ 73
Chapter Five:
   Bridging the Gaps ~
   *How to Make the Difference Work
   for Your Family Business* 91
Chapter Six:
   The Value and Richness
   in Diversity ~
   *How to Appreciate Your Fellow
   Family Business Member*............... 111

Acknowledgements

I never could have written this book without the help and guidance from a multitude of people – all of whom helped me develop over the years and brought me to this awesome point in my life and career. I'd like to take a few moments to publicly thank them here.

Thank you to my family, especially my grandparents, for giving me the opportunity, knowledge, and experience that only a family business can offer. I'd like to give a special thank you to my grandmother. Gramma Faye, you showed me how to be a businesswoman in a field of men and how to come out a winner. Thank you.

Thank you to my father, for being the most incredible mentor a daughter could ever have. You have guided me without judgment, supported me, and have always been there when I needed you. I love you.

Thank you to my mother, for showing me the importance of family away from the business. You lifted me when I was down, supported me through any decision, and guided me both personally and professionally. Mom, I miss you every day.

Thank you to my best friend, my husband, for your incredible support, love, and patience. With you by my side, I know I can do anything. The relationship and love we have built over the years is as strong and magnificent as the homes you build for your clients. You truly are my foundation. I love you.

Thank you to my two awesome kids for teaching me what life is truly about. No matter how hard the day is at the office or on the road, you are always there to remind me that fun and happiness are the most important things that life has to offer. Thanks for always keeping my perspective in check. Rachel, you will always be *my* Buttercup, and Kev, you are and will always be "da bomb"!

Thank you to a very incredible lady, Christine Corelli, who has unselfishly offered her guidance. You were a huge inspiration for me while changing careers. CC, you are the best.

Thank you to the many colleagues who have helped in the development of this book and my growth as a professional, including Ron Bliwas, John Ward, Roberta Miller, Doreen Marose, and Yolanda Ridley Scheunemann. Without all of you, my career would never have been what it is today. Also, I'd like to give a heartfelt thanks to Tom Abendroth and Lillian Bjorseth for offering their technical expertise on key issues in this book.

Thank you to Dawn Josephson, my incredible editor, for keeping me on task and helping me accomplish my goal of writing this book. You were always there for me, even though I'm sure you had other tasks to do. You always made me feel like I was your only client.

Last, but certainly not least, thank you to my dear friend Marlene Rubenstein, whose encouragement and love is never-ending. You literally would give me your last nickel and the shirt off your back. Everyone should have the gift of a friend like you.

Introduction

After being involved with my own family's business for nearly twenty years and consulting with countless others for the past five years, I have gained great insight to the dynamics of a family business. I've experienced firsthand the joys and frustrations and the triumphs and setbacks that come from working with the ones you love.

I also learned during those twenty years that family businesses have issues unique to them. The main challenge, however, was that when my family searched for answers to the many family business questions we encountered, none could be found. And the few answers we did find didn't sit well with certain family members. Back in the 1980s, the only seminars or books that addressed family business issues were so theoretical that they weren't much help at all.

When my family sold Beltone in 1997, I had the luxury of three choices:

1) I could get a job with another company;
2) I could be a full-time stay-at-home mom to my two children, or
3) I could supply other family businesses with the answers I was longing for and that I had to learn on my own.

I opted for choice three.

In the years since my family sold the business, my passion has been to give other family businesses tactics and tools that are workable, non-theoretical, and useful to help them advance their business and enhance their family relations. Although the large family businesses will benefit greatly from the strategies presented in this book, I wrote *From the Kitchen Table to the Conference Table* for the small to medium size family businesses, as these are the companies that drive our economy and contribute to our country's success. It is a book that you can read during a weekend so you can face Monday morning with real-life, workable, put-to-use strategies that won't take a lot of effort yet will yield great results and change your life instantly.

I've used each of the communication techniques in this book myself and have taught them to my clients with great success. Even though my communication style and behavioral tendencies are very different than my other family business members, I have learned how to interact with each person to gain maximum benefit. I realize too that improving communication with others is an ongoing process; therefore, even today, I am still dedicated to improving family relationships within my own family, as well as within other people's families.

For example, my father and brother are very detail-oriented people, which I am not. I prefer to look at the big picture rather than the details. With the strategies and tools in this book, I now am able to communicate with both my father and brother at their level and with their style. For my dad, I communicate with him by listening to his in-depth explanations and by asking many questions. For my brother, I communicate with him by focusing on the minute details that I would normally consider irrelevant. To him, they're very important, and I respect that viewpoint during every interaction with him. Just because we communicate differently doesn't mean we can't communicate at all. My other brother is much like me. But even with him, I have learned to adjust my communication style for improved communication. I've learned that I can sometimes come on too forceful for his liking, so when I communicate with him, I slightly tone down the passion behind my words.

Chances are that your family has similar dynamics. Some people are reserved, while others are outgoing. Some people are detail oriented, while others could care less about details. Some people speak with passion, while others appear more subdued. No one style is right, and we need all these behavioral preferences to make a family unit strong.

With the assessment tool in this book, you'll learn how to identify your own communication style as well as that of others. And with the strategies and techniques presented, you will learn how to communicate with everyone in your family business in a way that is productive and beneficial to both the business and the relationship. You'll know what to say, how to phrase it, when to say it, and what to look for in a reaction. In no time, you'll be able to read everyone you meet and adjust your communication style to build great relationships.

In the end, ***From the Kitchen Table to the Conference Table*** will help you make all your relationships harmonious ones.

Chapter One

The Good, the Bad, and the Ugly of Working with the Ones You Love

The majority of family business members agree that running a family business can be very rewarding as you share your successes with your loved ones. Additionally, they experience a level of trust in the workplace that only a family business can afford. However, those same people will also reveal that working with the ones you love has the potential to put a strain on both the family relationship and the business, as people's expectations of family members in the work environment are radically different than they would be of others. Whenever a family business has strain, the stress rubs off on all the family members, which can result in a feeling of "doom and gloom," both at the office and at home. Perhaps this is why the average life span of a family business is only twenty-four years.[1]

Before we go any further, let's review some basic facts about family business. As you read these, I challenge you to think about two things:

1) The power that family businesses hold in the United States, and

2) The daunting failure rate associated with family business.

- The greatest part of America's wealth lies with family-owned businesses.

- Approximately ninety percent of all business enterprises in the United States are privately held (family-owned), and nearly thirty-five percent of Fortune 500 companies are family firms.

- Family businesses account for seventy-eight percent of all new jobs created, sixty percent of the national employment, and fifty percent of the gross domestic product.

- Fifty percent of family-owned businesses have spouses, siblings, or cousins involved in the business.

- Nearly seventy percent of all family-owned businesses fail during the second generation. For those that do last, the numbers are not encouraging. Nearly eighty-eight percent close shop during the third generation, and ninety-six percent are gone by the fourth generation.

- Twenty-five percent of senior generation family business shareholders have not completed any estate planning other than writing a will, eighty percent want the business to stay in the family, and twenty percent are not confident of the next generation's commitment to the business.

- Sixty percent of succession breakdowns are attributable to relationship problems among family members.

The facts are bittersweet. While there are many advantages to working in the family business, such as freedom and financial rewards, many problems unique to the family business arena often arise, placing undue strain on many family relationships.

When asked, family business owners and members cite the following items as being the most stressful. What's interesting is that each of the items listed is a small aspect of one larger concern: communication/relationship issues. See how many you can identify with:

 *Financial Concerns*

Everyone has different ideas on the business finances and family member compensation.

1. For example, one family shareholder may need more take-home income, so he or she may desire greater dividends paid out to the shareholders. Another family member may prefer to reinvest in the business to see more growth. Since these two people have different financial outlooks, conflict could result.

2. Additionally, who gets paid and how much is another huge issue. Some family members may feel that all siblings, cousins, etc. should be paid the same salary (after all, there should be no preference shown from the parents, right?), whereas others may think that the oldest should get paid the most, with the remaining salaries falling in line with birth order. Still, others may think that they should run the company "like a company" and compensate all employees, family or not, based on the job they are doing and their performance. When beliefs are not shared, tension rises and family members turn against each other.

3. Another issue could be that the controlling generation who is "semi-retired" or fully retired is still receiving compensation from the firm, but not contributing to the daily operations. Some firms can

afford this, but others may not, as it adds overhead without the additional needed production they would get from a contributing party.

➤ Financial Concerns in Action

A hearing aid dispenser in Florida owned and operated four local offices. The four-store business was very successful in terms of the number of hearing aids they were fitting – in the top 2% of the franchise. Working in the business were the owner and his wife, their two sons, and the younger son's wife.

After thirty years of marriage, the owner and his wife, whose marriage always had its ups and downs, decided to get an amicable divorce. However, because the four offices were large and spread out, the family decided to split the offices among themselves and all remain in the business. Here's what happened:

The owner, his ex-wife, son number one, and son number two and wife were in the business. This means that four separate households were receiving income from the business. Each of these households was accustomed to a certain lifestyle, and they wanted their income to sustain that. They were each pulling a substantial amount of money out of the business. Although they were a sizable business in the hearing aid field, they still had trouble supporting all of the parties. All of the salaries serving the key managers/owners were "fixed expenses" or overhead and created an enormous financial breakeven point. Very quickly, they were no longer able to support themselves and the business, and the business ended up bankrupt.

 *Estate Concerns*

For the business to continue into future generations, an estate plan is necessary. Unfortunately, few family business owners want to address their own mortality. But the sad fact is that when the family business owner dies, the government takes a large percent (currently up to fifty percent) of the person's estate, less a one-time exemption (currently at one million dollars). To put it in a simplified and better perspective, if your mother owns a business worth $10 million and passes away in 2004 or 2005, the government taxes the estate $4,500,000 upon her death (($10,000,000 - $1,000,000) x 50% = $4,500,000.). Since most families can't afford to pay that amount, often times they're forced to sell the business in order to pay the taxes.

The good news is that tax laws are in the midst of change. As of the writing of this book, the current death tax rate is decreasing while the exemption is increasing on a schedule through 2009. It will be up to the current government administration to make laws following the 2009 stipulated death taxation. Regardless of the tax law that you are dealing with, estate planning is vital for all family businesses, as it protects the asset base that your family has built up.

There is another current law that allows people to gift up to $11,000 per year, per person, tax-free. The exact amount is increasing over time. Everyone who has a substantial asset base where death taxes will fall into play needs to be gifting the maximum amount to trusts or individuals yearly. You can do this in the form of stock from the business or cash.

➢ **Estate Concerns in Action**

Such a situation actually happened with my family's business, Beltone Electronics. The key owner, my grandmother who was in her 80s, was in failing health. Being children of the depression, she and my grandfather didn't feel comfortable passing stock down through the generations. So after my grandfather's death and more than fifty years of ownership, my grandmother alone was a seventy percent shareholder of this large corporation. If she were to pass away with that extent of ownership, her estate would have to pay the government a sizeable amount of money (in the tens of millions of dollars). As a family, we reviewed our options and decided to sell to another company in order to liquidate her assets in the then attractive market, as it was a good time to get maximum dollar for the business. Had she passed away without this type of planning, Beltone may have suffered dramatically, or we would have had to sell the business to pay the estate taxes, putting us in a possibly unattractive market in terms of selling conditions.

Why are family business members so hesitant to do estate planning? Again, it comes down to communication. Family business members:

1) May resist addressing their own mortality.

2) May not want to treat each member of the junior generation differently. As such, they do nothing at all. Some may worry that if they treat children differently in the business, they will have to deal with a child's uproar.

3) Children in the business may not want to admit out loud that they do not like a stepparent who joins the business, or parents in the business may not want to admit that

they do not like a child's spouse who is in the business.

4) May have had a great financial loss in the past that clouds their financial and estate planning judgments today.

 *Succession Concerns*

While the senior generation wants only the most qualified people to become the next business leaders, they often have a difficult time choosing between the various family members. Rather than create tension among the family members, the senior generation often agonizes over the decision and puts it off for as long as possible.

The larger issues revolving around succession include:

1) The parents or senior generation may not want to choose between their children; therefore, there is no clear vision of the future and everyone waffles. In extreme cases, those in the junior generation may start vying for positions.

2) The senior generation may view those in the junior generation as either currently incompetent or in need of major professional development. Some may even believe that the children will never become competent. As a result, the seniors put more pressure on the juniors, creating additional stress.

3) The senior generation's spouse may like his or her status in the family and community, and may covertly discourage succession planning in order to keep that status.

Similarly, the spouse may not want the business leader to retire and be home during the day.

➢ Succession Concerns in Action

Two brothers, Howard and Joseph, owned a chain of hardware stores in Minneapolis. Howard had 60% company ownership and Joseph had 40%. Both brothers were married with families. While no other family members played an active role in the business, Howard's son, Peter, had an MBA degree and did show some interest in possibly joining the business at a later date.

During January of their fifteenth year in business, Howard died during a freak snowmobiling accident. He owned the majority of shares of the business, but he did not have a succession plan in place. As a result, his wife, Marjorie, who had no business experience, took over his shares and began managing the company.

Unfortunately, it was quickly apparent that Marjorie was not a good leader, nor a good judge of people. In addition, she didn't trust her brother-in-law, as her husband had always told her how Joseph was a good behind-the-scenes guy and not a good manager.

Because of Marjorie's poor hiring and marketing decisions, combined with her refusal to work collaboratively with Joseph, the hardware store chain began to suffer. Soon, profits and customer satisfaction were at an all time low. Had Howard done some succession planning, perhaps his son, Peter, who had some business experience, could have taken over the stores, thus saving both Marjorie and Joseph lots of tears and frustration.

 *Family Concerns*

Challenges often arise in the family and business when a clear boundary is not drawn between the family system and the business system. Some family members may bring problems from home into the office, and vice-versa. Doing so creates unnecessary stress as family members feel that they never have a break from the office. In other instances, family members may treat and talk to each other in a way that is inappropriate in the office. For example, a sister may say to her brother, "You never could complete a project and you still can't." In these cases, the issues are deep-rooted relational problems.

Other common issues regarding family concerns are:

1) The family is so comfortable with each other that they conduct meetings too casually and not like a business.

2) The family members know how to press each other's "hot buttons" and do so in the office, just as they would at home.

3) The family members react to business challenges just as they do to personal challenges, which may include yelling, storming out of the room, name calling, etc.

➢ *Family Concerns in Action*

A family business in Louisville recently had a situation that caused a major uproar. The family business members consisted of the father, two brothers, and one sister. The middle son, "John," was married and had a young daughter. Everything seemed fine, and when everyone was together they appeared as a normal, all-American family.

Word soon got out, though, that John was having an affair with the business's office manager. As if such a situation isn't difficult enough, what made it even more stressful was that the rumor mill didn't stay within the office. Since so many family members worked with John, he experienced undo pressure for his actions both at work and at home.

The phrase "what goes on at work stays at work" couldn't work here. And while John was certainly out of line with his affair, his whole family complicated matters by discussing his behaviors and dealing with this issue at work and at home, eventually escalating the situation to enormous magnitudes.

 *Organizational Concerns*

Family business owners often build the company without a solid blueprint in mind. As they bring more family members into the mix, defining who does what task or job gets clouded. That's why defining roles and assigning jobs carefully, along with delegating authority and assigning accountability, are vital. If a business fails to do so, family members can get in each other's way or step on each other's toes. When there is no business blueprint, people start taking on many roles, which often cross over to someone else's duties. Hence, when there is disagreement, emotions and tempers can flare. In other families, people may not want to confront others and potentially hurt their feelings, so they choose to say nothing, causing the business to stall.

When working in a family business, people face additional organizational challenges due to the following communication issues:

    1) Everyone in the business wears multiple hats, and many times those roles overlap with each other. Without communicating

who does what, stress and tension are inevitable.

2) Some family firms have the family members make all decisions together as a collective unit. This is a highly inefficient decision making strategy, as it pulls people without knowledge or experience into realms of the business they are unfamiliar. It may also create inefficiencies as the family members are taken away from their jobs to help handle other areas.

➢ *Organizational Concerns in Action*

One of my clients hired me to help create an organizational structure for their staff, which included the family. When I began learning about the company, I saw that the father was trying to train his three children, whose experience in the business ranged anywhere from six months to fifteen years, by having them participate in making group decisions on almost every business issue – large or small. For the large issues, inexperienced members who lacked full understanding of the business were influencing the decision, causing much animosity among more senior members. It wasn't uncommon for an "inexperienced kid" to convince the father to move the business in a questionable direction.

For the small issues/decisions that needed to be made, having all family members join together to decide on an issue pulled members away from more important tasks. Additionally, the company had no role definitions, so all the members were functioning and doing the same job. As such, they had a lot of crossover and even more challenges.

To help, I set up an organizational structure for them, complete with specific role definitions and job descriptions, authority specifications, and guidelines on when certain members should be called on and for what. This created efficiencies and helped family members get along better, thus helping their business through the challenging times they were having within their industry.

Communication & Behavioral Concerns

Sometimes, family roles cross over to business roles when they should not. For example, when a mother joins the business, she may automatically want the children to report to her even though she is not the senior business member. On the flip side, when children join the business, the senior or controlling generation may not allow them, although unintentionally, to transcend their childhood roles. They may still view the newly arriving junior generation as those eight-year-old children who pouted when they didn't get their way.

Other commonly cited issues include:

1) Siblings may have a negative impression of each other personally, and that may hinder professional impressions as well.

2) Some family business owners may believe that the oldest child or the oldest son gets the business no matter what, even though another son or a daughter is more competent.

➢ *Communication & Behavioral Concerns in Action*

A family business in Miami, in a male-dominated industry (contracting), called me with many challenges. The family members consisted of a very domineering father and four children: two eldest daughters, a middle son, and a youngest daughter. All the children were married with children of their own.

The father expected the son to join the business right out of school, which he did and worked there for over 25 years. The eldest daughter had interests elsewhere in the business world. She eventually proved to be a phenomenal businesswoman (stronger than her brother). After 20 years in another industry, she joined the family business.

Immediately, the father made it clear that the son would inherit 40% of the business, and the daughters would get 20% each. This created an incredible amount of animosity among the siblings because of the perceived unfairness, especially in light of all the other children believing that the eldest daughter could run the business much better than the brother. They now are at the point where all the daughters think poorly of the father and the son, and they have trouble working with them.

The Root of All Challenges

Regardless of the issue or challenge, whether it's large and overwhelming, as some of this chapter's examples have been, or small and manageable, as all family businesses routinely face, you can resolve the issue and move on, provided that you have communication in place. In fact, each of the family business concerns listed becomes a challenge when communication is absent. If family members knew how to better communicate with each other about such topics as finances, estate planning, succession planning, organizational structure, and family/business perceptions *in the beginning*, before the problem got out of control, they could have greatly reduced and/or managed the existing problems.

Unfortunately, most family business members are unable to communicate about sensitive or heated subjects without ending up in some kind of argument. One person may yell while another may shut down, and yet a third may simply storm out of the room. Each person reacts differently, and no one understands why the others don't see the situation his or her way. While it's true that every family and every company group has disagreements, when you mix family members with business issues, the conflicts are more intense and more frequent. Family members know how to push each other's hot buttons, and they can do so freely.

With this in mind, many family business members wonder if it's possible to have a family firm where the members work *harmoniously rather than disparately.* They yearn for a way of addressing heated topics with family members in a manner that does not impede on the company's success. Fortunately, there is a way that family business members can transform communication conflict into a positive force that promotes business growth and productive relationships.

The Process

In the following chapters you'll discover how knowing, understanding, and using various communication skills, forums, and techniques can improve your business and family relations and your company's success. You'll learn why regular communication sessions (both formal and informal) are important for your family firm's future, as well as how to conduct meetings and what to address.

In addition, you'll learn how to identify and understand different communication and behavioral styles, how to pinpoint your preferred style as well as your family members', and how to communicate with each style type for maximum results. Learning these communication strategies is important, because the real secret to family business success is being able to communicate effectively with anyone at anytime. Armed with this new knowledge, you'll be able to "read" someone in minutes and ward off many communication problems before they start. In the end, you'll gain a deeper appreciation for each of your fellow family business members, no matter how opposite from you he or she is. So, regardless of how strained your family business relations may currently be, you can now lay the foundation for high performance and business growth.

Action Items

- On a scale of one to ten (with ten being the highest/easiest), rate how easy you think it is to get along with each of your family members. Write down your answers in the below chart.

Family Member	Difficulty Factor

- In this next step, review your pervious chart from page 29 and list those family members who scored above a five (6-10). This identifies those family member(s) you view as being the easiest to work with in your family business.

Easy to Get Along with Family Member	Difficulty Factor

- In this step review your pervious chart on page 29 and list those family members who scored below a five (1-5). This identifies those family member(s) you view as being the hardest to work within your family business.

Hard to Get Along with Family Member	Difficulty Factor

- Last, write down the specific challenges you face in your family business or members who you think fuel the challenge(s)? Write his or her name next to the challenge. Did you give that same person a low relationship rating in the previous question?

Challenge	*Family Member*

- Keep these business challenges and people in mind as you read.

Endnotes

[1] Dyer, W. Gibb Jr., *Cultural Change in the Family Business.* Jossey-Bass

Chapter Two

Family Meetings ~
The First Step to Improving Family and Business Relations

As we have just revealed, families who work together and live together have unique challenges that most other families don't face. While they have more opportunity for closeness, they also have more opportunity for disagreement. In order to balance the needs of the family and the needs of the business, family business members need to establish sound business practices that enhance not only the business's economic future, but also the family's happiness.

Running any business smoothly requires a great deal of skill, expertise, and decision-making. Families who are successful at business treat the business like a business, and they match people and tasks according to their natural skills and expertise. For example, if a child who is a "people person" wants to join the business, he or she would likely excel in a sales type position but flounder in a research or task oriented role. Likewise, successful family businesses often delegate the decision making process to those people most adept in the area that the decision needs to be made. For instance, if a junior member is not experienced enough to be part of a major decision, he or she may sit in on the decision making process for educational purposes. This junior member might even offer suggestions regarding the issue, but he or she would have less of a say in the final outcome.

Realize, however, that this process works only when strong communication is in place. That is, regardless of a person's position, skill level, or decision-making authority, he or she needs to keep other family members and employees in the loop of what is transpiring in the family business. Such communication is vital for success. Every family is reminded of this whenever miscommunication causes problems. Taking time to deal with issues before complications occur helps guarantee a smooth running operation with minimal conflict.

Many families have found that holding regular family meetings in addition to other business meetings have fostered good communications and have helped reduce potential conflict. Family meetings can be held monthly, bi-monthly, or seasonally, depending on how many people are involved and how complex the issues or organization is. However, regardless of how often the family decides to meet, it's best to schedule the meetings on a *regular* basis. When the meetings are built into the business routine, the family begins to rely on them for information and development.

Types of Meetings Typical for a Family Business

A number of situations, both within the family and the business, require formal meetings with family members and others. While the lines separating one type of meeting from the other may occasionally seem blurry, some "traditional types" of meetings exist, which have proven to work in successful family businesses.

- **Board of Director Meetings** – These meetings assure the integrity of the company's proposed strategic direction, CEO and top management accountability, and the succession process. The Board of Directors may be made up of family and non-family members; however, family business experts suggest that the board be composed of non-family members to add additional professionalism and an accountability factor to the family business members.

- **Shareholder Meetings** – These meetings are strictly business related. They exist essentially to ratify buy-sell agreements, make director selections, and reaffirm their vision and statement of ownership purpose. Other topics may include bonus structures, benefit discussion for employees, P&L review, and other strictly business topics. Also, not all family members are shareholders and therefore would not belong in a shareholder meeting.

- **Day-to-Day Operational Meetings** – These meetings address the daily work-related challenges that any business faces, such as marketing issues, cash flow, personnel, etc.

- **Family Meetings** – These meetings, which include *all* family members, discuss business *and* family issues. They are a great venue for discussions on succession and future plans for the business in general. They also help educate all family members (inside and outside the business) on business issues, challenges, and successes. Family meetings can help put a family vision into place and encourage family communication. In essence, the purpose of family meetings is to enlighten the family on the business, review and educate members on financial statements, and deal with family/business issues such as succession planning, estate planning, financial planning, and communication and relationship issues/problems.

When Family Meetings are Absent

Family businesses that don't incorporate family meetings into their operating procedures can suffer, both financially and emotionally. While the family members may think everything is progressing smoothly, likely they have unresolved issues stewing underneath that hamper future business and future relations. For example, if a sibling team works together and each has hidden negative feelings towards the other, those two individuals won't work as well together and probably won't be able to give their best effort to the business. Since by their nature family meetings encourage communication, a regular family meeting could help alleviate tensions among family members. Other problems that typically result from not conducting regular family meetings include:

- Family challenges fester and drive family members away from each other;
- No one knows what other departments or family members are doing in regards to the business;
- The "grapevine" runs rampant;
- Many family members could feel they must continually "watch their back;"
- The organization is not uniform and often goes in multiple directions at once.

The Advantages of Family Meetings

Having regular family meetings is just as important as holding business meetings where you cover day-to-day operational issues or shareholder issues. Such meetings enable all family members to better understand the business's direction and current challenges. And when everyone is on board with the company's goals, communication between people is usually better. Other key benefits of conducting a regular family meeting include:

- Gives strength to the family unit and keeps the family together;
- Helps members solve problems in an open forum;
- Allows for constructive debate of pressing issues;
- Enables everyone to hear information at the same time;
- Dispels misconceptions;
- Avoids backstabbing / politics;
- Gives one voice to the organization; and
- Provides constructive input to advisors.

Although not mandatory for a successful outcome, meetings that involve *all* family members, including spouses and children, have the added benefit of helping everyone feel like he or she is a part of the team. The younger members get the added advantage of learning how adults make decisions by observing the discussions at the meeting and observing the results of the decisions. Regular meetings also help the family plan for the future, which can help alleviate possible upcoming challenges, thus saving time, energy, and money.

When Someone Says, *"I Don't Wanna!"*

When trying to set up family meetings for the first time, you will most likely encounter one or more family members who don't want to participate or who don't see the benefits of formal family meetings. Fortunately, you can get people's buy-in for the family meeting concept by utilizing the following strategies:

1. Introduce the idea slowly so no one views it as threatening. Sometimes people resist the idea because they don't want to get too formal and they don't want to add any more to their workload. Indicate that the family meeting can be extremely

beneficial and add efficiency in many cases. Point out that family meetings help to address issues in a way that "nips them in the bud" in a short period of time rather than have the issues fester silently and possibly grow into bigger issues that are harder to resolve. Realize, though, that the meetings could be inefficient and add to the workload if you experience constant interruptions, if key people are not present, or if no one prepares prior to the meetings. Should those things happen in your family business, you may need to bring in an outside moderator to intervene. (See Outside Moderator section.)

2. Ask those who oppose the family meeting idea what challenges they see working with the family. Educate them that these are the types of issues that get resolved in family meetings.

3. Sometimes people expect too much from the meetings. Families may think they can solve problems in a few hours that have gone unresolved for years. While positive expectations are good, too high of expectations can slow progress and add frustration.

4. Some families attempt to accomplish too much in one single meeting. That's why several shorter meetings may be more effective than one long one. If the meeting goes too long people get tired, tempers may flare, and poor decisions may result.

5. Some family meetings are done as family retreats, which brings fun quality time into the mix with the whole family. At these types of family meetings there are activities for the kids while the formal meeting occurs. Afterwards, you can have planned group activities for the whole family to enjoy.

Conducting regular family meetings will take effort, but the rewards are well worth it. Family meetings encourage communication and build family strengths, which in turn will bring strength to the business.

The Five W's to Family Meeting Success

The following are important points to consider when deciding how to organize a family meeting. They are the five W's of meeting planning.

Why: *Purpose of Meeting*

Clearly state why you are meeting and what you want to accomplish. Meeting on a regular basis helps to create a smooth running operation and a closer family unit. However, if meetings drag out with no "success" (as defined by the pertinent issues discussed), no resolution of issues, or no new plans created, family members may stop wanting to come to them. If this is happening in your meetings, ask yourself and the family:

- Are the small, less important decisions being saved for the meeting and the more important decisions being avoided or being decided between family meetings? If this is the case, examine the content of your meetings. Are you addressing the members' needs? If you have sensitive or tough issues to address, don't plow right into them. Instead, tackle the smaller, easier issues first to gain immediate success. Doing so will also show members that the meetings are valuable and that you can work well together as a family unit. If it is still too difficult to resolve issues, consider bringing in a moderator to help. Whatever you do, don't give up, as the problem will still fester in the background. At the end of each meeting, do a debriefing session to assure that all members are happy with the outcomes.

- Instead of meeting on a monthly basis (which is the most frequent that family meetings should be and usually only if you have big issues or a timeline to deal with), could a more flexible schedule be proposed, like meeting bi-monthly or quarterly?

Who: *Attendance*

Decide who should attend the meetings and what each person's role will be (i.e., moderator, note taker, meeting leader, etc.). Prior to setting up the first meeting ask "What is the purpose of the family meeting?" Answering that question will determine which family members should be included. To help you decide who should be at the meeting, review the following list and make a decision based on what will work for your family. Who attends your specific meeting will be based on many factors, including your family business' dynamics, the sophistication of the discussion items, and each person's comfort level.

- First, consider which family members are currently in the business as well as which are not in the business but directly affected by the decisions made regarding the business. This includes all siblings, cousins, aunts, uncles, etc. who are impacted by business decisions. For example, if your father owns the business and only you and your sister work in it, you may want your mother in the meeting, but not aunts, uncles and cousins. However, if your father and uncle own the business, then the aunts and cousins might be in attendance. Also consider retired members of the family who are impacted by business decisions.

- Spouses of family business members. Some families are comfortable with this; others are not. One advantage of having spouses in attendance is that they get to hear the information for themselves and can form their own opinions about events, rather than having to hear the "filtered" information second-hand.

- Children beginning at a specific age as determined by the family. This allows kids to learn about the business before they are old enough to work in it. Younger children may not be able to sit still long enough for the meeting and may become disruptive. Once a year you can hold a special meeting including the children so they can learn the business philosophy and the family history as it relates to the business in a fun atmosphere.

Where: *Location of Meeting*

Choose a quiet, comfortable location with minimal interruptions, *away from the office*. All members must be able to relax and focus on the matters at hand. Because family meetings have the potential at times to get emotional, you need everyone's full attention with minimal distractions. Since meeting at the office is not the best option due to potential interruptions, consider meeting at a private meeting room. Some family businesses conduct their meetings at their attorney or accountant's office when they want a professional atmosphere with no distractions. Make sure each location has all the necessary tools, such as pens, paper, tables, chairs, grease board, calculators, calendar, etc. Realize that holding the meeting at a family member's home is not the best location. For example, if you hold the meeting at your home, and your brother has an issue with you, he may be "on guard" for the entire meeting, never quite feeling comfortable enough to share his concerns on your turf. As such, he won't be as productive at the meeting. Holding the meeting on neutral ground is the best option.

When: *Frequency of Meeting*

How often you meet depends on the family and complexity and severity of issues. Whether you decide to meet monthly, bi-monthly, or quarterly, commit to it regularly. Begin and end each meeting at specific times. Don't accept people breezing in late, announcing he or she has to leave early, and then insisting on jumping ahead to his or her part of the agenda. This is too disruptive to the family and the issues. A good way to start is to first establish meeting guidelines such as logistics, how people can address each other, how to stay on track, what to do when there is disagreement, etc. Some of the meeting guidelines relating to logistics are as follows:

- How to handle those who arrive late or leave early;
- How much time between announcing a meeting and the actual meeting;
- How to handle disagreements when they occur;

- How to treat each other inside and outside of the meeting;

- If people are always late, ask the family if a better time could be chosen;

- If one person has a habit of coming late/ leaving early and/or disrupting the agenda, then ask that person to be the meeting's chairperson.

What: *Meeting Agenda*

Agree on an agenda prior to the meeting and follow it. The last thing you want is for a discussion to suddenly shift to what color Mom and Dad should paint the house. If your meetings often get off the related topics, consider the following:

- Remind the family of the meeting's purpose and get back on track;

- If the new, sidetracked discussion is indeed important, ask the group if they want to take the time now to discuss it and delay the original topic until later, or if they want to schedule the new topic for the next meeting.

- Appoint someone to do the minutes and track what occurred, who agreed to do what, and by when. Also make sure everyone is doing what he or she agreed to do prior to the meeting. Too often, meetings have too much "shooting from the hip." Everyone needs to do his or her homework beforehand and come prepared. If you suspect that no one is thinking about the topics before the meeting, consider these questions:

- Do they have enough information regarding what is going to be discussed? For example, if you're going to talk about whether the company should subsidize some of the college tuition payments for the children who will be entering the business, then make sure others have access to the costs and how it will affect the business' bottom line.

- Is the agenda self-explanatory and does it put people in the correct frame of mind? For example, if the agenda states, "Communication Challenges and Discussion" it may not be clear what the discussion will be about or it may cause people to become anxious prior to the meeting. However, if the agenda says "Communication improvement discussion led by an outside team building specialist," then people are clear about the topic and will come ready to work.

Finally, at the meeting's end, sum up the results and agree on the next meeting's time, location, and future discussion subjects. As you do, go over all key discussion items and decisions, if there were any. If any action items came out of the meeting, make sure they have a person's name attached to them as well as a date for completion or follow up. Highlighting and logging the actions and dates assures that they are clear and gives them a better chance of getting completed. (See agenda on page 54.)

Choosing a Chairperson

Every meeting needs a Chairperson – someone to set the tone of the meeting, keep the meeting on task, and provide leadership. Many family businesses appoint Mom or Dad, or the primary controlling business member, to act as chairperson, which is their natural role. In reality, though, any family member can chair the meeting.

One effective way to handle the chairing of the meeting is to rotate the chairs. This gives every family member an opportunity to lead, which helps in his or her personal development as well as organizational skills. However, when the proposed issues to be discussed are tough, or if you suspect that tempers will flare during the meeting, then you need to get a family business facilitator involved. Additionally, if you are coordinating family meetings for the first time, you may want a facilitator to chair the first few meetings in order to get the family going and set the tone for this new kind of meeting. The facilitator can then turn the chair over to the family to continue, unless a hot issue arises that needs a facilitator again. Whoever acts as the meeting's chairperson, his or her main responsibilities include:

- Organizing the agenda;
- Including everyone in the discussion;
- Handling conflict;
- Defining and assigning tasks;
- Encouraging group participation;
- Listening to other viewpoints; and
- Wrapping up the discussion.

If you do opt to have the primary controlling member, such as Dad or Mom, chair the meeting, realize that group participation may become limited. Some family members may have the tendency to sit there and agree with Mom or Dad, yet not follow through with what was said or agreed to. This is when another chairperson and/or an outside moderator may be needed.

When an Outside Moderator is Necessary

During any family business interaction, conflict is inevitable. Depending on the topic, tempers may flare, people may storm out the room, or some people may simply "shut down." While those in non-family businesses may be able to control their emotions and remain "professional," in a family business situation, emotions can occasionally win. You have, after all, spent your whole life with these people, crying with them, laughing with them, and letting your emotions freely show. Just because you're in business together won't override all those years of family moments.

If emotions run too hot during your family meetings, an outside moderator is most likely necessary. Many family firms use outside moderators to manage conflict and keep the meeting on track. They feel that an objective outside person adds the structure their meetings require.

When choosing an outside moderator, make sure the family members collectively select and approve the desired person. This is important, because you want the outside moderator to be a good fit with the family members. If one or two people strongly disagree with the chosen person, conflict and mistrust could result. A good outside moderator will be someone who:

- Has family business know-how;
- Is a knowledgeable facilitator and is able to utilize assessment tools if needed;
- Is a good listener and a clear communicator;
- Knows how and when to use group decision making tools;
- Can effectively monitor and enforce rules of behavior during the meeting;

- Is sensitive and able to manage emotional vulnerability;
- Knows how to manage conflict collaboratively;
- Can set a tone of cooperation and brainstorming;
- Exhibits a positive attitude;
- Is objective and neutral to the family members and the business; and
- Is adept at adult teaching skills.

You can find a family business moderator by asking other family businesses for referrals, or by joining a family business center at a university and learning and/or meeting people who offer assistance. Currently, over 180 family business centers exist nationwide. If none are in your area, look online for family business moderators. Realize that you don't have to choose a moderator who is in your local area. Outside moderators routinely fly out to clients' locations to facilitate meetings. Additionally, many times "out of towners" are better received by the family members, especially in small towns where the family is well known.

Before deciding on a moderator, "interview" the person. Your first encounter with the moderator will likely be over the phone, so gain some comfort there. Plus, over the long haul, you will likely engage in a lot of phone work with the person, so make sure he or she can communicate in a non face-to-face venue. Once you're comfortable on the phone with someone, ask him or her to meet you for an interview.

During the interview, have the entire family present. Find out how he or she works with family businesses. What is her philosophy when working with families? How does he moderate? Does she get all opinions? Does he encourage the family to come together on decision? Does she help create small successes first to bring the family together? Ask for references, and then actually check them. How do other family businesses rate the person? Has the moderator helped them with similar issues that you are experiencing? Realize that due to the confidentiality requirements of some family businesses, the moderator may not always be able to give references. In this case, give the moderator a specific scenario and ask how he or she would handle it.

Have a list of all the questions you'd like to ask, and ask each potential moderator the same questions. This ensures that you're comparing apples to apples. Above all else, you and your family must feel that you can trust this person. In order for your moderator to be successful, you will need to share your issues with him or her, and trust is the key to doing that. Finally, remember to base your judgment of the moderator's individual expertise. Just because he or she may work or have worked for a large and prestigious organization doesn't mean he or she is right for you. A solo practitioner is just as competent as a big firm and is often more effective due to the "personal touch" he or she will give you.

Working Together

Outside moderators work with family businesses in a number of ways, depending on the needs of the family *and* the needs of the business. The moderator you choose needs to be able to tailor his or her services to meet your company's goals. For example, an outside moderator can have a role as a formal, objective facilitator, or he or she can be someone the family brings into the fold as an extended consultant and coach, helping resolve issues in and outside of family meetings. Family advisors are comfortable in either scenario, as well as everything in between.

Regardless of how formal or informal the moderator is with the family, the scope for family business consulting can go as deep as working with the family on major issues, to simply leading a family meeting. For example, when a family business asks me to help them through some major issues, I begin with a research stage. (Note: depending on the exact situation the process may vary.) The research could be as informal as conducting individual and confidential meetings or interviews over the phone, allowing me to learn about each person and his or her feelings about the business, the issues, and each other. Or it can be something more formal, such as having the family fill out a written survey coupled with the interviews. With the family's confidential information in hand, I am then able to lead them through the family meeting process, assuring the most rewarding meeting experience. We usually begin by establishing some meeting guidelines that the family produces. Then we move into the findings of the interviews and research – what is working great within the family and business as well as which areas we need to address. I can then facilitate the resulting conversations, assuring that each person is heard and that the pressing issues are discussed. The usual course is to tackle small issues first and gain success, thus showing the family that they can work well together towards a resolution. The family learns that they can build a foundation of success so that when the big issues arise, they are more equipped to handle them.

In a simpler situation where a family just needs a facilitator for a particular issue or to mediate a disagreement, I come in to just lead the meeting. Generally the up-front research is not as in depth as described above. Usually one or two contacts give me the information needed, such as what prompted them to bring me in and what issue or goal they'd like to resolve or accomplish. Before the meeting we discuss what goals and outcomes they desire, as well as why the way they have been doing things in the past hasn't worked. By understanding their successes and failures, I can adequately direct and lead them in the meeting setting. I then come to the meeting with an agenda and use facilitation exercises or techniques to help the family accomplish their goal. Many times, this is all a family will need. They are able to conduct their own meetings after they resolve the issue or attain the goal.

In general, facilitation is used when a family needs someone who doesn't get caught up in the family or business's roles and who can assure that each person gets a chance to express his or her ideas. Some facilitation techniques might include breaking the family members into smaller groups to gain ideas or, after setting up rules and guidelines for everyone to follow, facilitating a conversation to assure all people at the table are heard.

One family business brought me in to facilitate a discussion on succession planning. After doing some research, I learned that this family business had some more immediate issues that needed addressing before we could dig into succession planning. The family members (fifteen total) weren't communicating well with each other and couldn't agree on anything. We decided that each person would do a self-assessment to understand his or her communication and behavioral styles. Then a short presentation enabled everyone to embrace the differences that were in the room. An awesome thing then occurred – people began appreciating the differences in each other. This allowed them to understand the best way to communicate with the others and better identify the natural leaders.

For instance, one of the family members, "Bob," was extremely detail oriented and worked closely with his brother, "Norm," who was more of a visionary. Because of their different behavioral styles, you would have thought they were speaking different languages when communicating. Bob learned that Norm prefers only hearing bottom line information, yet he was always filling him in with details. Norm would always do other tasks while Bob spoke to him which disturbed Bob. On the flip side, Norm learned that when talking with Bob, his conversations had to be more structured and clear, and include the "between the lines" information that he used to think was a waste of time. Once the communication issues were presented and learned, the family was able to successfully move into succession planning, and a clear leader came forward.

Another company I worked with that had communication problems had a different underlying issue – lack of trust. Because of this lack of trust among family business members, everyone simply did whatever they thought was right, even if it was at odds with the other family members. During three sessions with facilitation, the family determined what was needed in terms of their meetings and communication. The family then established management meetings, shareholder meetings, and family meetings, none of which they ever had before. This helped them determine a direction for the company, which led them to work closer together towards the same goal, thus creating an atmosphere of working together. Slowly, they began to trust each other, and the company's productivity and profitability began to grow.

Family Meetings Work

In any family business, the family meeting is an important tool to keep the lines of communication open, all family members on board with current goals and objectives, and relationships among family members strong. Unfortunately, those lines of communication can only go so far. Each person also needs to know *how to communicate* and *how to understand* each other in order to make family meetings, as well as day-to-day interactions, more productive and stress-free (something we'll discuss in the remaining chapters).

Action Item

As you prepare for your first or next family meeting, use the following checklist to ensure your meeting is a success.

1. List what you think you would have to do to get a family meeting to work in your company or improve (if you are already conducting family meetings).

2. Where is the best place to conduct your meeting?

    _____at private meeting facility
    _____at someone's home
    _____at attorney's office
    _____at accountant's office
    _____other: _____

3. Who would be the best moderator?

_____ Family member: _____

_____ Rotating family members

_____ Outside moderator: _____

4. What should the family discuss?

_____ Family vision

_____ Family communication

_____ Roles of family members

_____ Knowledge passed onto family members, both in and out of the business

_____ Development of family areas needing development

_____ Rules for when family members can enter the business

_____ Cash flow

_____ Estate planning

_____ Tax planning

_____ Succession planning

_____ Other: _____

5. How often should family meetings be held?

_____ Monthly

_____ Quarterly

_____ Annually

6. How should final decisions be made?

   _____ Majority rules

   _____ By the senior generation

   _____ No action unless consensus

7. Plan an agenda for your family meeting (See example page 54.)

Sample Agenda

Quarterly Smith Family Meeting
November 7, 2004
Location: We-Serve-Em-Well Hotel and Resort
Pleasantville, NC

"Coming Together to Stay Together"

Dress - Business Casual

7:30 AM	Union Salon AB **Continental Breakfast**
8:00 AM	Union Salon AB **Welcome and overview of day** Julie Smith **Financial Statement Review** Robert White, accountant
9:00 AM	**Communication** Laura Michaud, Family Business Expert
10:30 - 11:00 AM	Break
11:00 AM	Union Salon AB **Communication Improvement** **Brainstorm Session** Laura Michaud
12:30 PM	Club Terrace **Lunch**

1:00 - 5:00 PM Union Salan AB
    Old Business
- Buy- Sell agreements
- Director approval

    New Business
- Meeting debriefing and next steps

Chapter Three

From Business Savvy to People Savvy -
How Communication and Behavioral Styles Affect Business Success

Whether interacting with family members at home or on the job, we each have a preferred style of communicating. How we communicate is a part of who we are, and our communication style is usually second nature – something we rarely think about and that we "just do."

Likewise, our behavioral styles (how we say things and how we behave) are also second nature and often dictate how we communicate. As such, many people find it easier to associate with and understand others who are just like them. Those who are different can come across as "difficult" to work with and can cause frustrations to arise.

To be successful in a family business, family members need to understand several factors regarding behavior and communication. That is, they need to 1) understand their power, 2) understand how their behavior affects others, and 3) understand themselves. Only then can people accept other people's behavioral and communication styles and work harmoniously together to produce results.

Let's go over each point in detail.

1. *Understand Your Power*

Family members in a family business have a certain degree of power within the organization, and many times they don't realize how strong or powerful they are. This power can range from financial power to organizational power, and it's often directly related to the individual's position in the family itself (i.e. son of owner, niece of owner, etc.). For example, when I started at Beltone, I was 24 years old. My father, who was an incredibly astute man, encouraged me to work outside the business for another company before bringing me into the family business. When I did join Beltone, I started at an entry-level position where I worked under the COO (a non-family member), who, at the time, felt threatened by my mere existence.

I, of course, had no idea of the COO's feelings. I considered myself an easy-to-work-with person and had no intention of threatening anyone. But when I came into the corporation, the COO was nervous because he was extremely close with my father and saw me as the boss's daughter, who could affect his job, career, and "standing" with my father. Because I had a stronger bond with the boss than he did, the COO feared I might change things and "rock the boat." The COO understood my power; I still did not.

The COO's assignment was to expose me to all the different departments of Beltone so I could better understand the company. Then the three of us – my father, the COO, and myself – would determine where my talents and skills would be best suited. Since he felt threatened, the COO decided to stick me in an office where I was to read manuals and articles in order to learn the industry and the history of the company. He instructed me to learn every fact possible about hearing aids – where they were developed, how the parts were made, how they were fitted on patients, etc. While I certainly needed to know the background of hearing aids, I was missing the experiential learning that was supposed to take place along with the COO's assessment of my abilities. The bottom line was that I was frustrated that my skills were not being used in a capacity that positively impacted the company.

At the six-month mark, my father asked me over for dinner one Sunday evening. During the meal, he casually asked me, "How's it going at work?" I respectfully told him that I was learning about the industry, but that I felt my talents and the company's money were being wasted on my training. Perplexed by my answer, he questioned me further. I then explained what my daily training program consisted of. It was then that I learned the exact instructions my father gave the COO. Since the COO was my boss, I never knew what my father's instructions were to him. All I knew was what the COO told me to do, which I did for much longer than I would have in any other company. After my father learned what the COO assigned me to do, my father quickly corrected problem. The COO revised his "training schedule" and begrudgingly assigned me more appropriate tasks.

That day I realized my power. I had a direct link to the guy who had all the votes.

Whether you're a succeeding family member or you have children who are going to join the business, make sure that you and your children know your/their power and what it means.

Those in a family business are often told that they're "born with a silver spoon in their mouth" and that that's where their power really lies. But is that true? Sure, many people born into a family business have instant jobs, but often the newly arriving member has to work extra hard to prove him or herself to the company and/or employees in order to gain the credibility that would normally go with a particular person in the job he or she is performing. Those born into a family business have to prove to outsiders that they're not just lucky; but they also have talent and abilities to be a productive employee. I understood the importance of learning the industry and the company's history, but I also knew my training and professional development was lacking. I possessed ability to offer something beneficial to the business, yet I was not being directed or allowed to utilize my skills.

All of this plays into the power issue. When a new family member comes into the business, people will respect "who that person is" based on the fact that he or she is family (and has an element of control over the employee's future). They will then act accordingly, even if the family member is in an entry-level position. In other words, people will jump when the new family business member asks them to jump, just because he or she is related to the boss. This doesn't mean the new family business member is competent to give direction.

Therefore, you need to have humility when you come into the business, because people don't know your ability. And, in some cases, family members are put into jobs that might be above their current ability. But when you know your power, you can devote your energy to showcasing your talents so your "silver spoon" becomes less apparent. As such, you'll develop a respect for others, and they, in turn, will respect *you* for *you*.

2. Understand How Your Behavior Affects Others

Everything you do and say at the office and at home affects other people in your life. What you may think is a harmless or unobjectionable behavior may very well offend someone else. That's because we react to others based on our own communication and behavioral style. The fact is that everyone has a part of their "make-up" that will bother others. But no one behaves certain ways for the sake of annoying people. We behave in certian ways because of who and what we are. So if what someone does bother you, it is likely because the other person communicates and behaves differently than you.

For example, in one family business I worked with, the owner's son, "Mathew," oversaw the accounting department. When he was there, he worked very hard. However, he took advantage of the fact that he was a family member. If he wanted to get his hair cut, he'd leave for two hours at lunch. If his wife had plans to go out in the evening, he'd leave work by 4 p.m. so he could watch the kids for the night. Mathew took advantage of his power, and his department knew it. As such, when 5 p.m. came around, everyone was out the door in his area. The reasoning was that if he could do it, so could they. Employees traditionally take their bosses lead, and his department was a shining example. Other departments would stay late or not watch the clock as much.

Granted, Mathew often took work home and worked very hard at home, but no one saw that. They only saw the behavior he demonstrated at the office, and that's what affected his team. Mathew is a perfect illustration of why we need to know how our behavior and our power affect other people.

So if you do something well, maximize it. That good behavior will cast a positive impression on others and will affect them positively. Likewise, if you have a family member who isn't good in sales and marketing, but you have a hole there and say, "Hey, John, you've got to help out in sales and marketing," you're going to have a mismatch. As a result, your family member is not going to be happy if he is forced in this position for long. Realize that sometimes, especially in smaller companies, someone may have to wear a hat he or she isn't perfectly matched for. The pain and frustration come when that person has to be in the position for too long. As others in the company notice the person-to-position mismatch, they may view him or her as incompetent, thus making it more difficult for that person to gain credibility. That's why it's important to know what you do well, to maximize what you do well, and to know how what you do and how you do it affects other people.

3. *Understand Yourself*

The key to realizing your power and understanding how your behavior affects others is to understand yourself. When you understand yourself, you can learn ways to modify your behavior and/or communication so you can be effective when you're interacting with others, whether they are like you or not. This is important in a family business, because you'll be interacting not only with family members, but also with non-family members who may or may not understand you and your behaviors. So by knowing your strengths and weaknesses in regards to behavior and communication, you can be better prepared to deal with people, whether you are interacting with your family during a conflict, managing employees, or dealing with a difficult colleague. When you know yourself, you can modify your presence or behavior in order to accomplish a successful communication or direction.

In the early 1900s, a researcher named Dr. William Marston conducted studies on people and their behaviors. The premise of his research is the remainder of this chapter's foundation.

- *Genetic Traits:* According to Dr. Marston, we are all born with genetic traits. You can call it DNA, or you can call it your personal makeup. Either way, it's what makes you "you."

- *Core Personality:* In addition to the genetic traits, we each have a core personality. Your core personality is who you are in a given environment. For example, if a child is born into a household that is very peaceful, and the child is by nature a very aggressive and assertive person, that child will still be aggressive and assertive in the household, but in a more toned down way than if he or she were raised in a more intense environment. The bottom line, however, is that a person is born with this personality trait, it will always be there – it is innate.

- *Observable Behavior:* On top of genetic traits and core personality, you also have what's called "observable behavior." These are the traits the outside world sees of your core personality. So when you are talking about "who you are" and what you see in other people, you're talking about observable behavior. You're not talking about genetic makeup or core personality, because those are beneath the surface and kept from the outside world.

Realize that your observable traits are situation-based. You may behave and communicate one way at home and another way at the office. You may also behave and communicate differently depending upon the people who are present. Behavior is flexible and dynamic, and it's based on your thoughts and beliefs at the given moment.

Now, behavior for those who work in a family business is interesting, because home and work thoughts and beliefs often intermingle. For instance, if you are in the middle of doing some succession planning with your family/business members, and all of a sudden the discussion gets intense because two siblings are vying for the CEO position, it's very possible that emotions may show in a way not typical in a traditional business environment. One person may start to cry, another may pout and moan, while yet another may swear and storm out the room. When put in a non-family business situation, these same people may stay composed and not show their emotions so openly. However, since they are with family, they're comfortable showing their emotions and not holding back. For each person, behavior comes out in different ways and for different reasons.

Over the years, many researchers have developed tests and assessment tools to identify various personality and behavioral types. The purpose of such tests is to help people improve some aspect of their lives. Two popular assessments exist whose purpose is to help people create better teams and improve communication. They are the Myers Brigg Type Indicator and the DiSC® Personal Profile System. I have used both of these assessments extensively, and they both give fantastic results. However, because of its ease of use and understanding, the DiSC Personal Profile System yields my clients the greatest results. When done properly or under a facilitator's supervision, the DiSC enables people to gain a better perspective of what make them *them*.

So, before we go any further, it's important that you understand what makes you *you*. That is, you need to identify and understand your core personality and your observable behaviors. By doing so you'll be better able to understand how you react in a given situation and with a given person, and you'll gain a greater understanding of other people's behaviors. With this knowledge, you'll interact with others more productively and will engage in less conflict with those who are unlike you.

The **Action Item** below is an assessment tool that will help you peel back the layers of your behavior. Should you want to conduct a more thorough assessment, refer to an Inscape distributor or call the numbers at the back of this book.

Action Item

The following assessment tool consists of 16 sets of four statements. In each of these sets identify those behaviors that are typically most or least characteristic of you. Read the four statements under each heading, and then rank them from 4 to 1, give 4 points for the behavior most like you, 3 points to the next most like you, then 2 points, with 1 point being the statement that reflects your least typical behavior.

Beginning with the "A" statements, enter the number you assigned to each in the appropriate box on page 71. Repeat the process for all "B," "C," and "D" statements.

Check your accuracy by adding the columns' totals together; they must equal 160. If they don't, recheck to make sure you have attributed all four numbers in each scenario.

Look at the Score Tally Box on page 71 to verify your most prevalent behavioral style. If two of the numbers are the same, you have a tendency to use both of these styles equally.

Family Business Behavioral Style Assessment

Rank each set, 4 points is the most like you and 1 point is least like you.

1. Report Formats

    _____A. I prefer a summary upfront with only key findings listed.

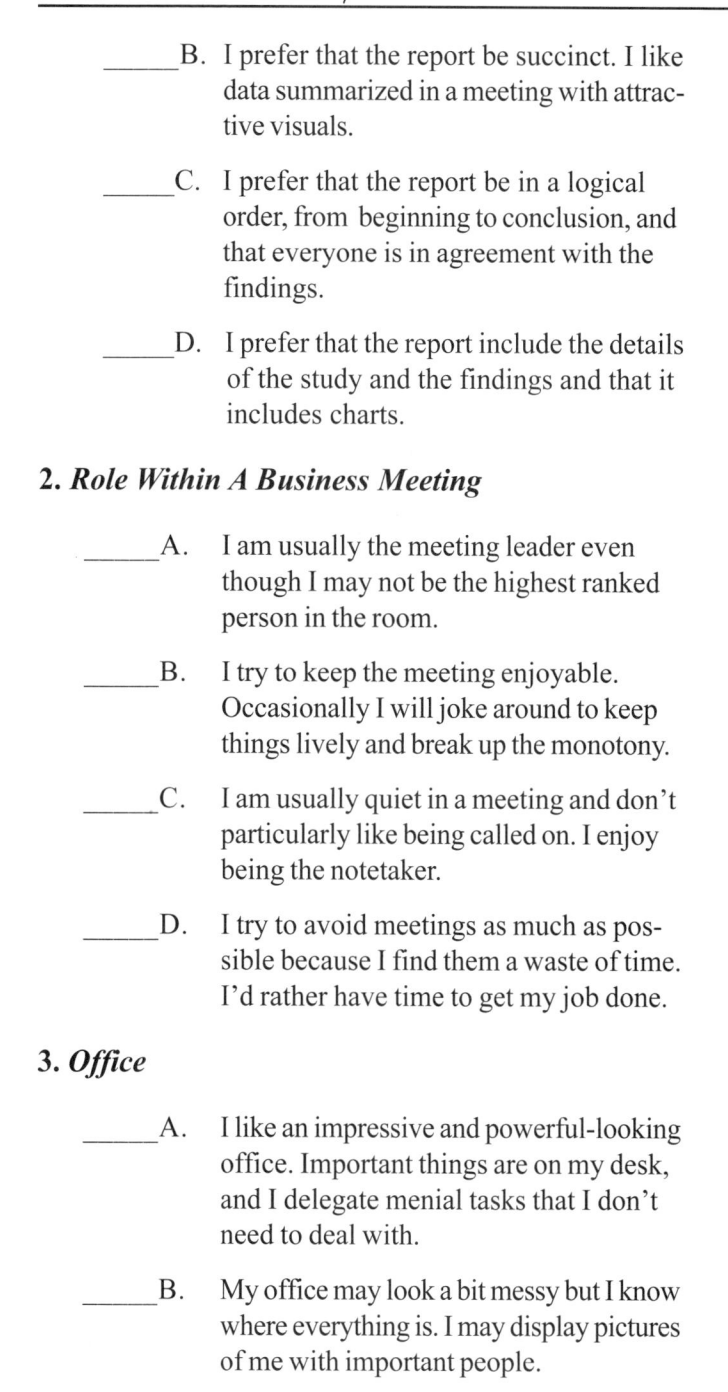

_____ B. I prefer that the report be succinct. I like data summarized in a meeting with attractive visuals.

_____ C. I prefer that the report be in a logical order, from beginning to conclusion, and that everyone is in agreement with the findings.

_____ D. I prefer that the report include the details of the study and the findings and that it includes charts.

2. Role Within A Business Meeting

_____ A. I am usually the meeting leader even though I may not be the highest ranked person in the room.

_____ B. I try to keep the meeting enjoyable. Occasionally I will joke around to keep things lively and break up the monotony.

_____ C. I am usually quiet in a meeting and don't particularly like being called on. I enjoy being the notetaker.

_____ D. I try to avoid meetings as much as possible because I find them a waste of time. I'd rather have time to get my job done.

3. Office

_____ A. I like an impressive and powerful-looking office. Important things are on my desk, and I delegate menial tasks that I don't need to deal with.

_____ B. My office may look a bit messy but I know where everything is. I may display pictures of me with important people.

___ C. My office has a warm feeling and is neat and orderly. I may display pictures of my family and pets around me.

___ D. I am very organized and know where everything is. I may display graphs or charts pertaining to the project I am working on.

4. *Business Functions*

___ A. If the function relates to my interests, I'll stay. Otherwise, I may come late or leave early.

___ B. I attend every function I can, as I love meeting new people. You never know where your contacts will lead you.

___ C. I prefer to blend in with the crowd and visit only with people I know.

___ D. I learn by observing in a business social setting, but would actually prefer to use my time in other ways.

5. *Out-Of-Office Activities*

___ A. If I'm not challenging myself in the office, I'm pushing myself on the racquetball court, mountain biking, windsurfing, or some other exhilarating activity.

___ B. I like to go out with my friends and family. It's the perfect time to enjoy them.

___ C. I prefer to stay home with my family. Hanging out at the house is just perfect for me.

_____D.   I prefer organizing things at home such as doing taxes, balancing the checkbook, organizing files, etc.

6. Handling Disagreements

_____A.   I'll let people know I disagree with them immediately. I'd rather not waste time pussyfooting around an issue. If I have to come on bold, I will.

_____B.   I let people respectfully know that I disagree with them. I won't make a big deal out of it. If they question me a lot, I may back down just to keep the peace.

_____C.   I prefer not to have disagreements. If they happen, I like to ignore them and hope they will go away.

_____D.   I don't like to address disagreements until I have researched the situation and possible solutions thoroughly.

7. Delegation Style

_____A.   I tell people what outcome I want and then let them do their job. I expect it to be done on time and correctly.

_____B.   I like to direct people by establishing an environment in which they motivate themselves to exceed.

_____C.   When delegating, I think out the logistics of the project. I then decide on the best people for the job and make sure they really want to do the task.

_____ D. I prefer to do the work myself so it is done right. When I do delegate, I describe exactly what I want done and by when.

8. Decision Making

_____ A. I can easily make decisions.

_____ B. I may initially hesitate, but then I listen to my gut to make decisions.

_____ C. I like to get a consensus from colleagues and subordinates before making a decision. That way decisions have buy-in right off the bat.

_____ D. I like to gather as much information as I can before making any decisions. The more I know, the better my decisions will be.

9. Risk Analysis

_____ A. If I think the risk will have a big payoff, I jump in without giving it much thought. If I miss seeing a consequence, I'll deal with it when it comes up.

_____ B. I rely on the positive side of taking a risk. I might occasionally miss some of the negative results that could occur, but those usually get worked out.

_____ C. I only take a risk if it's absolutely necessary, and even then I hesitate. After all, if something is working, why change it?

_____ D. I never take a risk until I do long-term and short-term risk analysis so that I can be assured of a successful outcome.

10. *When Introduced To People*

___ A. I always greet people with a firm hand shake to let them know they are dealing with someone with confidence.

___ B. I'm the touchy-feely type so I'd just as soon hug as shake hands.

___ C. When I greet people, I want them to know how genuine I am so I greet them warmly to make an instant connection.

___ D. I greet people with the least amount of fan fare, sticking to social protocol.

11. *Written Communication Style* (e-mail, letters, faxes)

___ A. I prefer e-mail, as I can get right to the point and messages are received instantaneously.

___ B. I prefer face-to-face. It's easier to "read" people this way and respond appropriately. Besides, it's also more fun.

___ C. I prefer communicating via the phone or face-to-face. I enjoy listening to people rather than reading something from them.

___ D. I prefer communicating through writing a letter. It allows me to fully express or explain my ideas and provide backup information.

12. *How I Sell Ideas*

    _____A. I get right to the point with the benefits and the idea.

    _____B. I promote the idea as much as possible to anyone who can influence its acceptance. In a formal setting, I would use attractive visuals.

    _____C. I would plant seeds privately to see if any one liked the idea and let it germinate on its own.

    _____D. I would gather data to prove that the idea is sound. Then I would present all the facts so that an informed decision could be made.

13. *Competitiveness*

    _____A. I love solving all kinds of challenges. Competition charges my batteries.

    _____B. If it's friendly competition, it can be fun. If it gets brutal, I am uncomfortable.

    _____C. I prefer not to have to compete. I am best just left to do my job without competition entering the equation.

    _____D. I don't like competition, but I can handle it as long as I have researched the situation and have lots of facts and statistics to back things up.

14. *Sales Call Preference*

    _____A. I prefer a salesperson who's a straight shooter and who gives me only the facts I need.

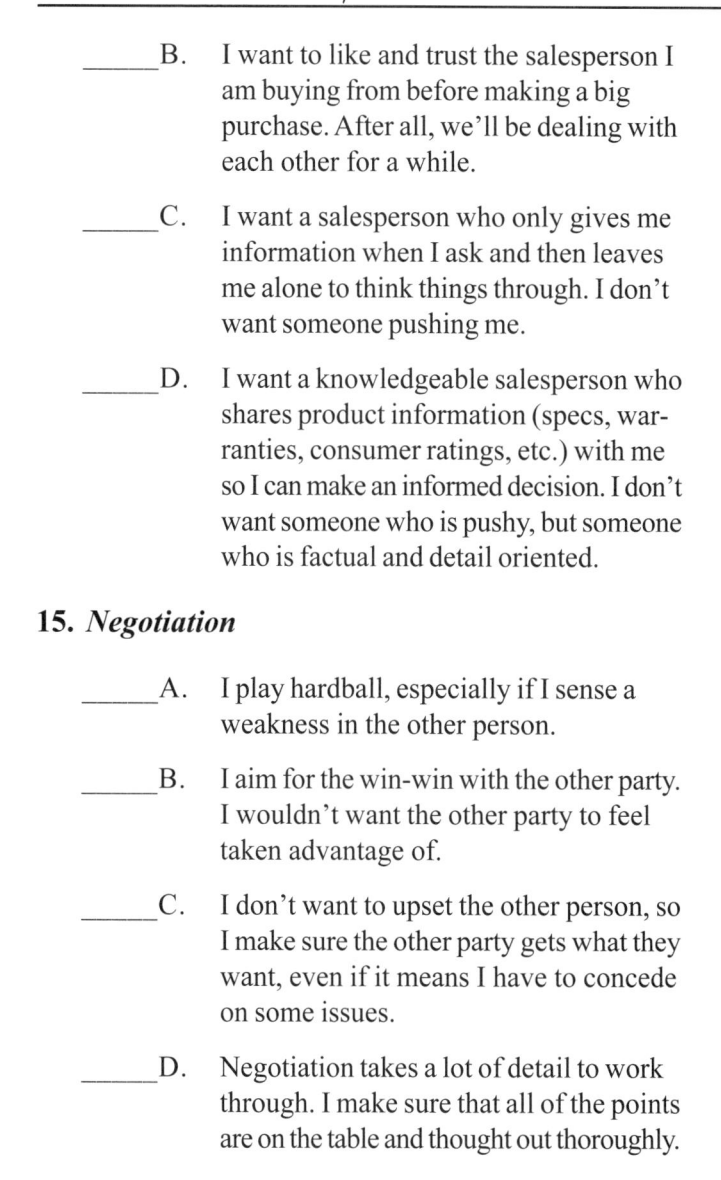

_____B. I want to like and trust the salesperson I am buying from before making a big purchase. After all, we'll be dealing with each other for a while.

_____C. I want a salesperson who only gives me information when I ask and then leaves me alone to think things through. I don't want someone pushing me.

_____D. I want a knowledgeable salesperson who shares product information (specs, warranties, consumer ratings, etc.) with me so I can make an informed decision. I don't want someone who is pushy, but someone who is factual and detail oriented.

15. *Negotiation*

_____A. I play hardball, especially if I sense a weakness in the other person.

_____B. I aim for the win-win with the other party. I wouldn't want the other party to feel taken advantage of.

_____C. I don't want to upset the other person, so I make sure the other party gets what they want, even if it means I have to concede on some issues.

_____D. Negotiation takes a lot of detail to work through. I make sure that all of the points are on the table and thought out thoroughly.

16. Voice Mail Messages

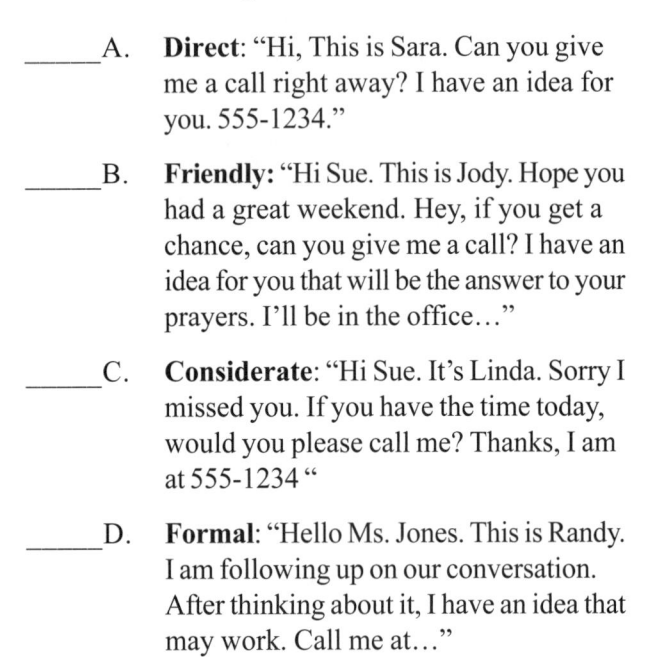

_____A. **Direct**: "Hi, This is Sara. Can you give me a call right away? I have an idea for you. 555-1234."

_____B. **Friendly:** "Hi Sue. This is Jody. Hope you had a great weekend. Hey, if you get a chance, can you give me a call? I have an idea for you that will be the answer to your prayers. I'll be in the office…"

_____C. **Considerate**: "Hi Sue. It's Linda. Sorry I missed you. If you have the time today, would you please call me? Thanks, I am at 555-1234 "

_____D. **Formal**: "Hello Ms. Jones. This is Randy. I am following up on our conversation. After thinking about it, I have an idea that may work. Call me at…"

Score Tally Box

For category heading, enter the number value you assigned to each satement in the appropriate box. (4 being most like you down to 1 being least like you).

Category Heading	A	B	C	D
Report Formats				
Role Within a Meeting				
Office				
Business Functions				
Out-of-Office Activities				
Handling Disagreements				
Delegation Style				
Decision Making				
Risk Analysis				
Introduced to New People				
Written Communication				
How Sells Ideas				
Competitiveness				
Sales Call Preference				
Negotiation				
Voice Mail				
Totals				

Scoring:

- Add the **Columns A, B, C, D.**

- Check that the totals of Columns A through D add up to 160. If your totals do not add up to 160, then check your addition and make the appropriate correction(s).

- Circle the total that yields the highest figures. You may find that two columns have equally high ratings.

Results:

- If your highest number is in ***Column A***, you are a ***Driver*** in your family business.

- If your highest number is in ***Column B***, you are an ***Impeller*** in your family business.

- If your highest number is in ***Column C***, you are a ***Stabilizer*** in your family business.

- If your highest number is in ***Column D***, you are a ***Careful One*** in your family business.

Chapter Four

Understanding You ~ What it all Means

With your new behavioral profile information, it's time to take a deeper look at what the categories mean and how they impact family business. As we go through each behavioral style, we're going to keep peeling back the behavioral and personality layers so you can understand the people you live with and work with better.

Let's begin by breaking the general behavioral tendencies into four quadrants.

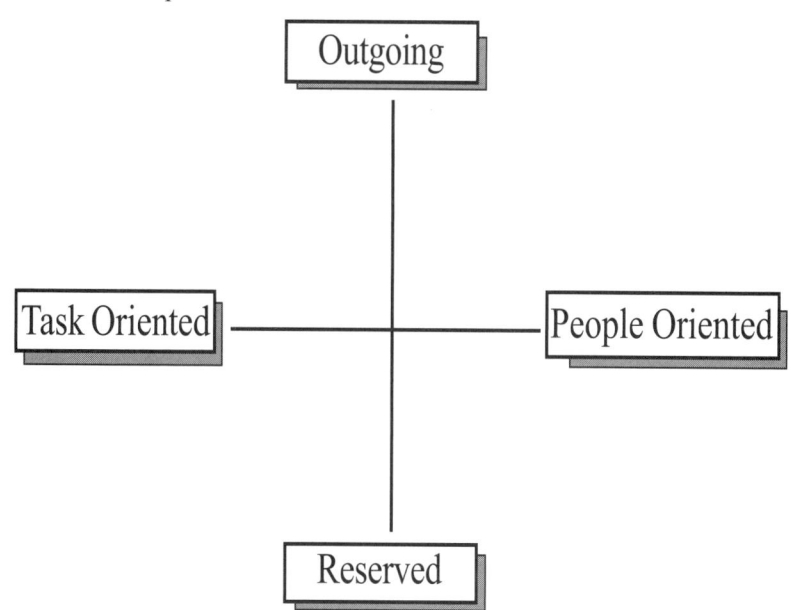

```
              Outgoing
                 |
                 |
Task Oriented ---+--- People Oriented
                 |
                 |
              Reserved
```

Adapted from Dr. Marston's DiSC Personal Profile System.

Obviously we can't pigeonhole people into a quadrant, but the diagram gives us an indication of where we are on each scale. Remember that each person is different, like a fingerprint. The mixture of characteristics and our strengths determine who and what we are. On one axis, people are either outgoing or reserved, and on the other axis, they are task oriented or people oriented. If we overlap the four behavioral styles of **The Driver**, **The Impeller**, **The Stabilizer**, and **The Careful One**, we end up with a more detailed Behavioral Style Quadrant Diagram (see figure below).

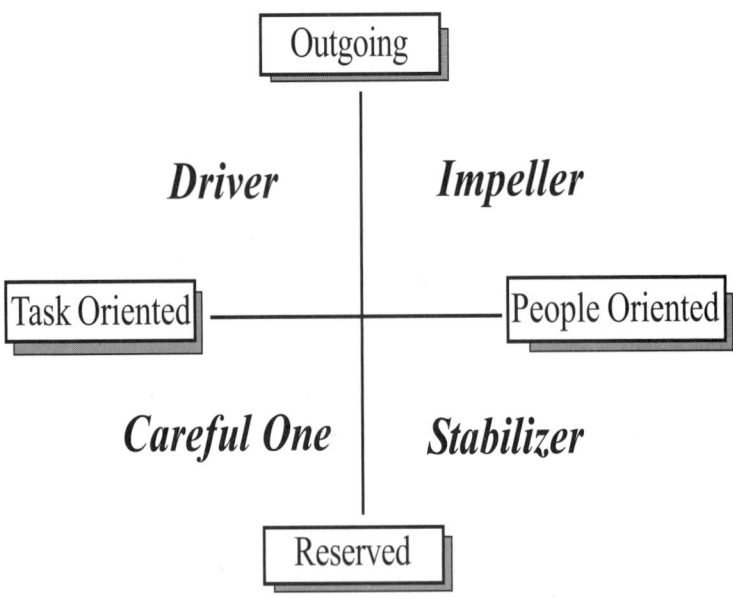

```
                    | Outgoing |
                         |
         Driver          |         Impeller
                         |
  |Task Oriented|--------+--------|People Oriented|
                         |
       Careful One       |         Stabilizer
                         |
                    | Reserved |
```

As you can see, Drivers are outgoing and task oriented. The Impellers are outgoing and people oriented. The Stabilizers are people oriented and reserved. The Careful Ones are task oriented and reserved. With that base knowledge, let's delve deeper into each behavioral style.

The Driver

One who drives; the person that urges or compels anything else to move onward.

Just as the definition implies, the Drivers "drive" the organization. They are the dominance people. They love overcoming opposition. Drivers are natural born leaders. They run things from day one. You will often find them determining the "play" on the playground, heading committees, and setting the stage for others.

A Driver's tendency is for immediate results. They're very decisive people. These people sometimes take action so fast that they don't see what's going to happen later on. Drivers are imperative to a successful organization because they are the ones who stick their necks out. They are the visionaries who are forging ahead and pushing the organization.

Challenge, power, and authority motivate Drivers. They like things fast and are the ultimate multi-taskers. As such, they love the Internet. Most Drivers would tell you that the Internet is one of the best modern inventions. Because they are natural multi-taskers, they expect others to be able to juggle multiple tasks with ease just as they do.

Drivers are very confident. They have a strong ego, and while they don't intentionally showcase their strong ego, people often sense it. Drivers are the kind of people who won't read a manual. They get something out of the box and they put it together without a second thought. Drivers also hate the status quo. They love change and don't feel powerful unless they're changing something. They have a strong self-confidence and love taking risks.

Drivers (as well as the other styles) have negative aspects relating to their style that they should be aware of. One area for improvement is that they often go ahead with a risk and many times don't think about the consequences. As such, others often view them as the "steamroller" or "bulldozer." Additionally, they're very impatient, and they can move forward without considering the initial steps needed to accomplish the task or the outcome. And, just like all people, Drivers have fears. Drivers fear a loss of control and will conduct themselves as a way to stay in control. They also fear being taken advantage of.

Snapshot of The Driver

Drivers Are:

- Direct
- Natural Leaders
- Daring
- Visionary
- Bold
- Risk Takers
- Bottom Line Oriented
- Confident
- Fearless
- Strong-Willed
- Efficient
- Fast-Paced

Others May Perceive Drivers As:

- Demanding
- Impatient
- Aggressive
- Domineering
- Blunt

How To Spot A Driver:

- Drives a power-car, such as a Mercedes.
- Talks on the cell phone while driving.
- Works on the computer while on the phone.

- Yells or barks orders at others.
- May be short-tempered, very confident, and demanding in speech.
- Does things assertively.
- Decorates their office with awards, trophies, and prestigious objects.

In Stressful or Extreme Situations:

- Will come on strong.
- Will walk away (or storm away) from situation.

> *The Driver in Action*

John is one of four siblings who works in the family business. Being the successor to his father, he wants the business to grow – and to grow quickly. At the monthly family meeting, he can't understand his siblings' lack of enthusiasm for starting the meeting, and he often wonders how the business is as successful as it is. He figures that all the success to date must be all due to his effort, and that's why he deserves to be the next in line for the CEO chair.

As he looks around the room at his siblings and other family members, he often just shakes his head in frustration. He watches his sister Marcia as she flutters from person to person and does nothing but make idle chitchat. He finally says to her, "This isn't a cocktail party. We're here to work, so it's time to stop the small talk."

He also notices that his brother Mark is in his usual spot at the table with pen and paper at hand, ready to take the notes of the meeting. John then looks towards the far corner of the room and sees his brother Brian diligently doing some calculations on his handheld calculator and furiously scribbling the results on a piece of paper. He knows that Brian has probably been in that corner working feverishly for the past fifteen minutes. Brian is always the early one.

"Come on Brian," John says. "We have lots to do. It's time to come and join us." With some hesitation, Brian turns off his calculator, gathers his papers, and joins the group.

Thankful that the meeting is ready to begin, John takes the lead and plows forward with the discussion.

The Impeller

> *One who incites to action or motion in any way.*

Impellers are known for moving others to action. These people love to persuade and influence others. They value relationships, because in their mind, nothing is better than enjoying people and accomplishing things with others.

Impellers are enthusiastic and entertaining, and they are involved in anything that has to do with people. "Sociable" and "persuasive" are the key words for Impellers. They express their emotions freely and are great charmers. They are usually great in sales or any field that has a lot of people contact. On the flip side, Impellers aren't the best listeners. They'd much rather be holding the conversation. In fact, an average person can talk approximately 140 words a minute; an Impeller can talk as fast as 400 words a minute. These are the people who run out of time on the voicemail. You can almost think of them as a coffee break waiting to happen.

Impellers are motivated by social recognition and relationships. The best way to sell to an Impeller is to build the relationship. Take them out to dinner, wine and dine them, and they'll often be on your side.

Impellers fear social rejection and disapproval, so occasionally you may see them give in to an argument just to keep the relationship happy and intact. They also tend to be impulsive and may lack follow through.

Snapshot of The Impeller

Impellers Are:

- Optimistic
- Great Communicators
- Enthusiastic
- Outgoing
- Friendly
- Animated
- Influential
- Charming
- Sociable
- Generous
- Persuasive
- Fun

Others May Perceive Impellers As:

- Emotional
- "Touchy-Feely"
- Self-Promoting
- Impulsive
- Talkative

How To Spot An Impeller:

- Drives a sporty, fun car.
- Can be the life of the party.
- Is confident in a room of people.
- Talks fast and usually with great animation.
- Decorates their office with pictures of themselves with famous people.

In Stressful or Extreme Situations:

- Begins overselling.
- May pout.
- May back down.

> ### The Impeller in Action

Marcia hates when her brother John tells her to stop talking, especially when they're at the monthly family meeting. This is, after all, the time for everyone to connect and catch up, and that's what she likes to do best. But since she doesn't want to upset her brother or strain the relationship, she gives in to his request to stop talking. She pouts as she takes her place at the table.

She often wonders how she's related to her three brothers, especially since they're so different from her. She gets along well with Mark (he is so agreeable, after all), but she always felt that Brian was quiet and shy, and she always wished he would open up more. And to her, John is too demanding and too focused on work and results. Marcia never understood why he was chosen to succeed their father in the business. She believes that John was never respectful of other people the way her Dad was. To her, a CEO needs to possess much better people skills than what John has.

The Stabilizer

One who makes stable or steadfast.

Stabilizers are the nicest, sweetest people you will ever meet. They love constancy, they're cooperative, and they're extremely loyal to the organization or the people they work with. Like the Impellers, they're people-oriented, but unlike them, they are reserved. They're very supportive in an organization. You couldn't have a successful team without them.

Stabilizers are great team players because they're calm, patient, logical, and loyal. They're great listeners. When you ask a Stabilizer to do something, he or she will always be receptive and jump right in to help.

Sincere appreciation motivates Stabilizers. They want to always know that they're doing a good job. Stabilizers dislike change. To them, change is extremely uncomfortable. If these people get divorced or lose their job, they agonize over it for a long time, much longer than any other style.

Stabilizers often take a long time to make up their minds. They're so nice that they don't want to alienate anyone, so they'll overanalyze every decision. They often put their own needs last and take on a *"whatever you want, I'll do"* mentality.

As a team player, these people have a strong concern for the group. As a leader, they will likely ask the group their consensus. They usually won't make decisions until they know how each member feels about things. They take a very methodical approach to things.

Stabilizers fear loss of steadiness, change, and unpredictability. Because of this they may resist positive change. Their areas for improvement are that they're overly willing to give and they may put their needs last. Sometimes they refuse to make changes because they fear their decision may make someone unhappy.

Snapshot of The Stabilizer

Stabilizers Are:

- Team Players
- Loyal
- Giving
- Kind
- Warm and Friendly
- Helpful
- Patient
- Good Listeners
- Methodical
- Stable
- Predictable
- Cooperative

Others May Perceive Stabilizers As:

- Passive
- Fearful of Change
- Complacent
- "Wishy-Washy"
- Too Nice

How To Spot A Stabilizer:

- Drives a practical SUV.
- Wants to always "keep the peace."
- Is loyal to the family, company, or the cause.
- Decorates their office with pictures of family.

In Stressful or Extreme Situations:

- Gives in.
- May accuse.
- Will act hurt.

➢ *The Stabilizer in Action*

Mark knows that his brother John means well and wants the company to grow, but he often thinks that John is too blunt and forceful, especially in a business setting. He'd much rather have his sister Marcia run the company, but he would never voice that opinion to anyone. The last thing he wants to do is cause conflict or change the way things are running.

So Mark comes to every family meeting with his usual pen and paper and painstakingly takes the notes so no one else has to. Although he has some good ideas on how the company can improve, he usually waits until someone asks for his opinion before he speaks up, and even then he presents his ideas cautiously, watching other people's reactions as he speaks. He doesn't want the company to change too quickly. Plus, he's very satisfied with the way things are going now.

The Careful One

One who is thorough and painstaking in action or execution; conscientious.

Careful Ones emphasize quality and accuracy. Many times they are your "bean counters." Data is so important to them that it's their life. In order to prevent overlooking any details, Drivers and Impellers need Careful Ones to be a part of their team. These people want to understand what information is available and break it down into workable chunks. They love details and feel that others will appreciate the details as well. When they send out memos, they will include all of the attachments to support their memo that, of course, the Drivers and Impellers don't read.

Careful Ones are detail-oriented. They're analytical in nature and very accurate. They usually over-prepare everything. They dislike conflict and deal with it covertly. Careful Ones are motivated by performance expectations. That is, you let them know what is expected of them, and they'll do it exactly as outlined. They like when others value their accuracy.

These people value detail, and they like a very businesslike atmosphere. While Impellers love working with and through people, Careful Ones don't like to stand around the coffee machine and discuss business. They prefer to work with their data. A quiet professional atmosphere is what they prefer. And unlike Drivers, Careful Ones actually read manuals and instructions.

Careful Ones fear criticism and emotional outbursts. They dislike emotional challenges and will actually stay away from situations where there are emotional outbursts. Their areas for improvement are that they're critical of themselves and tend to be very hard on themselves. They're also indecisive when they feel they don't have all the facts. They always want more data before they make a decision. As a result, their creativity and what would appear to be initiative could be hampered.

Careful Ones Are:
Snapshot of The Careful One

- Analytical
- Detail-Oriented
- Accurate
- Systematic
- Observers
- Rule Followers
- Perfectionist
- Fact-Finders
- Reserved
- Courteous
- Quality-Oriented
- Businesslike

Others May Perceive Careful Ones As:

- Critical
- Indecisive
- Rigid
- Restrained
- Controlling of their data

How To Spot A Careful One:

- Drives a car that has good consumer data and will often run the gas down to assure the gas tank is exactly 18.3 gallons.

- Enjoys balancing the checkbook.
- Has a process for everything and likes to describe it to others.
- Decorates their office with charts or graphs of current projects.

In Stressful or Extreme Situations:

- Can't decide.
- Begins emotional attacks.

➢ ***The Careful One in Action***

Brian hates going to the monthly family meeting because it takes him away from other important tasks. Even so, he attends every meeting and usually arrives anywhere from five to fifteen minutes early. The entire time, though, he's thinking how he'd much rather be at his desk working or doing research for one of his many projects. Plus, lately the meetings have had way too much conflict for his liking. He is much more comfortable dealing with problems on paper.

Brian sees his brother John as impulsive and can't understand why John doesn't use processes for his decisions. He thinks that by adding formal processes they would alleviate much stress and anxiety. He also wishes his sister Marcia would appreciate the data he collects for her. He gets frustrated that she rarely reads what he sends her. He gets along with Mark well because he feels that Mark appreciates the research and information he constantly provides.

As Brian takes his place at the meeting table, he's secretly resentful that he can't work on his charts and calculations anymore. He knows that paper calculations will yield him greater results than any group discussion.

Getting a Glimpse at Yourself and at Others

In the first chapter you identified those people with whom you get along and those with whom you don't. As you think back to those people, you should be able to identify them as having characteristics in one or two of the four behavioral styles. Are the ones you get along with most like you? Or do you get along best with the people least like you because you complement each other? Are the ones who give you challenges most unlike you? Or are you and your adversary so similar to each other that you vie for the same positions?

While we don't want to pigeonhole people into categories, because we all exhibit characteristics from more than one behavioral style from time to time, we can make a few observations.

- ***Drivers*** and ***Impellers*** tend to feel they are more powerful than the environment. That is, they feel that they can easily change things and improve them. For example, if a succeeding family member is a ***Driver*** or an ***Impeller***, he or she would come into the business, see how it was run, and then say, "I could run this place better. I could make some major changes here. Dad did alright, but I could do better." A ***Stabilizer*** or a ***Careful One***, on the other hand, feels that the environment is more powerful. He or she would come into the same situation and say, "I can learn from this. I'm going to see what's going on, and then determine if I should implement any changes." So there's a difference in the mentality people have based on their behavioral style.

- ***Drivers*** and ***Careful Ones*** look at their environment more on the pessimistic side, while the ***Stabilizers*** and ***Impellers*** feel more optimistic. In other words, ***Drivers*** and ***Careful Ones*** see things more negatively; they may be more apt to distrust people. ***Impellers*** and ***Stabilizers*** are more accepting of the environment and are more trusting of people. A way to look at the difference is that the ***Impellers*** and ***Stabilizers*** might wake up and say, "Good morning, God," while the ***Drivers*** and ***Careful Ones*** might wake up and say, "Good God; it's morning." Again, it's a difference of perception.

- ***Drivers*** and ***Impellers*** tend to stretch or even break the rules, while ***Stabilizers*** and ***Careful Ones*** work within the prescribed rules. For example, when you're negotiating a contract with a vendor, you know the industry norms and what is acceptable and expected in a client/vendor relationship contract. ***Drivers*** and ***Impellers*** will feel more powerful than the rules (environment) and will look for ways to improve what they have. They will find the loopholes in the contract to try and get more while paying less. ***Stabilizers*** and ***Careful Ones*** are more likely to work within those rules and abide by the norms. They will concentrate on the accuracy of the contract. As such, it may actually cost them a bit more for the same product or service, because they're working with the prescribed guidelines rather than challenging them. They don't want to leave their comfort zone.

The following graphic best summarizes the previous points.

Environment Perception As Seen
By Marston

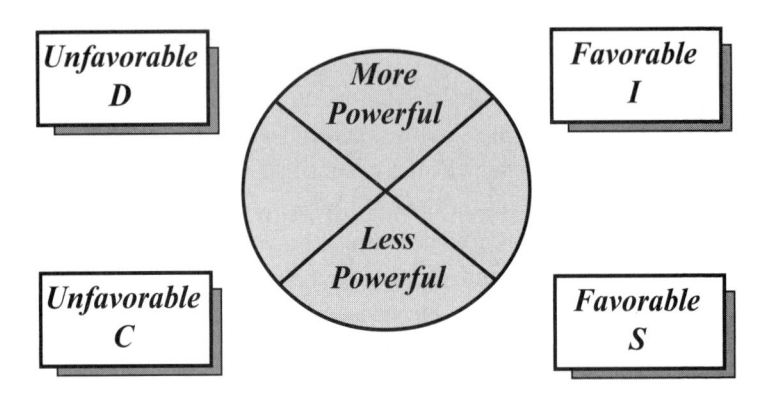

Unfavorable D	More Powerful	Favorable I
Unfavorable C	Less Powerful	Favorable S

Adapted from Dr. Marston's DiSC Personal Profile System

Action Items

- Go back to the charts you filled out in **Chapter One** on page 29. Think about the family members and the difficulty factors you indicated in chapter one. Now, next to each, write down the person's observed behavioral style. (As a reminder, the first two columns of information, Easy/Hard to get along with and Difficulty Factor, were completed in chapter one. Simply reuse that information.)

Easy to Get Along with Family Member	Difficulty Factor	Behavioral Style

Hard to Get Along with Family Member	Difficulty Factor	Behavioral Style

- Identify how you are alike and different from each member.

Family Member	How Alike	How Different

- Notice how these differences may be a factor in the challenges you indicated having.

Chapter Five

Bridging the Gaps ~
How to Make the Difference Work for Your Family Business

Now that you've discovered your own behavioral style, as well as that of your fellow family business members, you can better relate to each person with whom you live and work. But relating to and understanding people is only half the solution. The next step is to learn how to work effectively with the different behavioral styles so the business can prosper while keeping your family strong.

Realize that the behavioral styles you identified in the previous chapters are situation-specific, based on how you view yourself or your family members at work *or* at home. That is, a person may act one way at work and another way at home. In addition, that same person may act different depending on the situation at hand. So if someone is a Driver at work, he or she may seem more like an Impeller at home with the kids and more like a Stabilizer when interacting with the in-laws. While everyone will likely be strong in one or two behavioral styles and exhibit those traits most often, we are all multi-dimensional and may exhibit some of each of the four behavioral styles at one time or another.

For example, through my coaching, I once worked with a family business member who was a strong Driver. He was results-oriented, he came on strong with co-workers and family business members, and he was unforgiving in terms of business objectives. He also exhibited many traits of a Careful One.

He would get his mind on something and use every bit of information he could gather to sell his point. Even when others told him they disagree with his idea, he still would try to prove his idea right or drive it home.

A month after my work with him ended, I saw him at a convention with his wife, who did not work in the family business. I could hardly believe he was the same person. With her, he was sweet, giving, and kind. He catered to his wife and put her on a pedestal. While in the office he was a strong Driver and Careful One, with his wife he turned into a strong Stabilizer. It was an amazing change of character and a great reminder to me of how we all act differently in various situations and with various people.

Making the Differences Work

When we learn to understand behavioral differences between people, we can discover practical ways to work with the differences and to utilize each style's strengths, thus enhancing family business relations. By doing this, we instill a greater sense of teamwork in each member, enhance communications, and greatly reduce the stress and frustration many family business members experience.

With the behavioral groundwork in place, the company then gains a competitive edge in the marketplace. From a business perspective, this is important, because a successful organization requires all four behavioral styles to run things smoothly and to keep all departments and systems in check. For example, Drivers generate new business ideas and insist on results. Impellers go out and promote the ideas. Stabilizers assure the ideas get carried out and bring stability to the group. And Careful Ones cover the key details and assure the job gets done properly.

Without each of the four behavioral styles present, key aspects of the process wouldn't get done sufficiently, thus causing a less successful outcome. If your family business does not have each behavioral type represented in your mix, then you may want to consider hiring an outside person who can add some much needed perspective. If the budget is tight and hiring an outside person is not an option, then one person may need to take on the perspective of the missing behavioral style, even though it is not his or her main operating mode.

- *Drivers* generate new business ideas and insist on results.
- *Impellers* go out and promote the ideas.
- *Stabilizers* assure the ideas get carried out and bring stability to the group.
- *Careful Ones* cover the key details and assure the job gets done properly.

With this in mind, it's important to know what kind of behaviors to expect from others in a given situation, as well as how to interact with the various behavioral styles. Keeping these in the forefront during every interaction can help ward off many conflicts before they begin.

In Normal Situations...

- *Drivers* are in-charge and deciding. They direct and control the situation.
- *Impellers* are persuading and enthusiastic. They love working with people, and others generally respond positively to them.
- *Stabilizers* are supportive and friendly. They appear to get along with everyone, and people generally enjoy working with them.
- *Careful Ones* are cautious and quiet. They are conscious of producing good work and want to assure accuracy.

Under Pressure...

- *Drivers* will demand their way. They will get stern and firm as needed, many times coming on extremely strong. They may actually bully their way into getting what they want.

- *Impellers* will oversell their ideas. They will begin talking faster and will get anxious.

- *Stabilizers* will give in to others. They will back down and become even quieter than they traditionally are.

- *Careful Ones* will not make a decision. They will become even more indecisive when under pressure.

In Extreme Situations...

- *Drivers* will leave (or storm out of) the room. They will control the situation by leaving. If they're not there, the incident can't continue.

- *Impellers* will give up and pout. They will let others know of their dissatisfaction without causing additional conflict.

- *Stabilizers* will act hurt and make accusations. They will make others feel sorry for them and do what they can to prove that they were right.

- *Careful Ones* will make emotional attacks. They will cite their facts or data sources to further push the issue.

When Doing Financial Planning...

- *Drivers* set the big picture tone for the financial planning process. They determine the end result that everyone should strive for.

- *Impellers* make sure everyone is happy with how the planning is accomplished. They will stay away from the actual planning process and will review the objectives in the end.

- *Stabilizers* think up the details and the best plan of attack. They will set up the logical process and assure it is running on time.

- *Careful Ones* read and analyze the documents, trusts, etc. They will check to assure the numbers are working and lined up properly.

When Selling Their Ideas...

- *Drivers* get to the point quickly and without unnecessary fluff or small talk. They give the bottom line results and numbers first.

- *Impellers* take people out to lunch and engage in small talk before discussing the idea. This allows them to know their prospect and what their hot buttons are so that they can sell against them.

- *Stabilizers* give the details and then keep their distance. They allow others to mull over information and then regroup for consensus.

- *Careful Ones* give facts, figures, charts, and graphs to highlight the strong points of the idea. If the prospect is indecisive, they give more charts and graphs.

When Revealing a Setback to the Group...

- *Drivers* tell others what happened and how the situation can be fixed. They don't give long explanations of "why."

- *Impellers* tell others what happened and then assure them that everyone is going to pull through. They then offer ways the group can come together and fix the situation.

- *Stabilizers* first tell others that everything will be okay, and then alert them the setback. They explain why something happened and then gain consensus with everyone as to what can be done to fix the situation.

- *Careful Ones* first recap the steps that transpired prior to the setback, and then state the actual setback. They offer specific calculations or facts to prove that everyone can get back on track.

In a Meeting...

- *Drivers* will call the meeting to order and will set the meeting's tone. They will direct the meeting and make sure the pressing issues get covered.

- *Impellers* will socialize before, during, and after the meeting. They will want to keep the mood light.

- *Stabilizers* will take the minutes of the meeting. They will not offer input unless someone specifically asks them for it.

- *Careful Ones* will research items for the meeting. They will cite their findings to support any points they make.

When Choosing an Attorney or Accountant to Work with...

- *Drivers* will meet the person face-to-face in a business setting and ask the person key, factual questions. They will choose the person who appears the most knowledgeable and gives the best, to-the-point answers.

- *Impellers* will meet the prospective person over lunch or coffee. They will attempt to establish a relationship prior to asking business-related questions. They will choose the person who appears the most knowledgeable and social.

- *Stabilizers* will do most of the contact via phone. They will take detailed notes of every answer and compare the answers and mull over the information. They will choose the person who appears the most knowledgeable and who goes into the most detail.

- *Careful Ones* will research each person he or she interviews ahead of time and will come to the meeting with a detailed list of questions. They will choose the person who appears the most knowledgeable and who supplies the most supporting documentation of their credentials and expertise.

When Planning a Convention...

- *Drivers* spearhead the convention concept. They decide which conventions would be the best to go to, which market at those conventions should be singled out, what products would be best to take to the meeting, etc.

- *Impellers* make sure the location is perfect. They talk with the convention hall to sweet talk the best location. If there is any entertaining to take place, the Impeller will pick out the perfect venue to impress the customers or the prospects.

- *Stabilizers* take care of the details, like setting up the booth. They will ensure that the Drivers and Impellers have everything they need to be successful. They will make the travel arrangements, book the hotel rooms, etc.

- *Careful Ones* read the contract. They will make sure all details are covered. They will even research traffic pattern flows at a convention to assure the booth location is the best.

When Selling the Company...

- *Drivers* will seek out the highest bidder. They will sell to anyone who is willing to pay the right price and won't back down on any selling points.

- *Impellers* will try to form a relationship with the prospective buyer. They will want to ensure that the new owners will keep the company's original values intact.

- *Stabilizers* will give prospective buyers lots of information regarding the company's standing and past. They will often make concessions to keep the prospective buyers happy.

- *Careful Ones* will research each of the prospective buyers and will be prepared with a detailed list of points as to why the business should sell for a certain amount. If the buyer would offer less for the business, Careful Ones will have charts and graphs ready to back up the existing asking price.

When Dealing with a Lawsuit...

- *Drivers* will send all the information to their attorney and not bother with the details themselves. They then may cut off all communication with the threatening party and direct their attorney strategically.

- *Impellers* will want to talk to the people initiating the lawsuit to try to smooth things over. They will then forward the information to their attorney and will check in with the attorney weekly for a status report.

- *Stabilizers* will lament over the lawsuit and will wonder what they did wrong to cause it. They will give their attorney every document he or she requests, along with a long explanation of why everything was done a particular way.

- *Careful Ones* will dig up any and every piece of information related to the lawsuit, write out long and detailed statements, photocopy the documents in duplicate, and send one copy to their attorney. They will file the other copy in a safe location.

When Disciplining an Employee...

- *Drivers* will tell the employee exactly what he or she did wrong and how to correct it. They will be blunt and will come on bold if the employee, too, is headstrong.

- *Impellers* will first tell the employee how great he or she is in many areas. They will then state the issue that needs to be ratified. The may even minimize the issue. They will offer to help the employee in any way possible.

- *Stabilizers* will point out the problem and then will attempt to take the blame for the problem, as in "It's probably my fault for never telling you about this in the first place..." They will assure the employee that he or she is still very valued and appreciated.

- *Careful Ones* will send a multi-page e-mail or memo to the employee stating exactly what he or she did wrong, when the event occurred, why it was wrong, and what he or she needs to do to correct the behavior.

Strategies for Dealing with Each Type

Think back to the **Action Item** exercise you did in chapter four. In it you identified the behavioral profiles of your family business members. Chances are you identified a mix of Drivers, Impellers, Stabilizers, and Careful Ones. With some of them, you get along fine. You see eye-to-eye on many topics, and you communicate your ideas effectively with them. With others though, your relationship can be like an all-out brawl or a relationship of avoidance. You can't work together well, and you often leave a conversation in a state of frustration and confusion.

Each behavioral style exhibits certain characteristics that are foreign to the other styles, making it difficult for everyone to communicate harmoniously. However, when you're aware of each style's preferences, you can alter your communications approach as needed so the person's you're interacting with understands you and your expectations. Then, when everyone is "on the same page," so to speak, you can reach consensus and work together effectively. To help you better relate to your fellow family business members, keep the following communication strategies in mind:

When Interacting with Drivers:

- Be brief and to the point. Don't make small talk. If something doesn't pertain to him or her, it's better left unsaid.

- Don't drone on or focus on details. These people get bored quickly.
- Don't take what they say personally. They have a sharp, direct tongue and rarely think before they speak.
- Be sure of the information you give them. They may challenge your findings.
- Be ready for quick topic changes and incomplete sentences.
- Listen carefully. They will give big picture ideas rather than details.
- If you need more clarification or detail, ask for it. They will not offer it on their own.
- Look them in the eye. To them this is a sign of strength.
- Show them results rather than process.
- Keep the conversation logical and factual. Emotionally based reasons don't register with them.

When Interacting with Impellers:

- Ask them questions about themselves to develop rapport.
- Don't confront them. Rather, come to the table with win-win ideas.
- Be animated when you speak.
- Compliment them.
- Let them talk, and listen carefully.
- Guide the conversation to keep them on track.

- Let them have center stage.
- Offer to connect them with influential and/or famous people.
- Name drop.
- Learn what motivates them and use it when trying to sell your points.
- If you need something by a certain date, follow up with them regularly and remind them.
- Take them out to public places and develop rapport and experiences with them.

When Interacting with Stabilizers:

- Meet with them in their own familiar surroundings.
- Don't interrupt. Let them finish their long explanations.
- Ask them open-ended questions to encourage them to reveal themselves.
- Ask for their opinions on ideas and truly listen to them.
- Define goals with them.
- Do not insist on too many changes at once.
- If there is an upcoming change, alert them in small doses so they can get used to the idea as early on as possible.
- Watch to make sure they don't take on too much. Find out what else they are working on to ensure that you are not overloading them.

- Don't criticize. If you need to correct them, do it with compassion.
- Show them that you support their causes.
- Always smile when you speak with them.
- Don't tell them to see "so and so" for more information. Instead, introduce them to the person.

When Interacting with Careful Ones:

- Don't ask personal questions.
- Be specific with your answers and be prepared to back them up with facts.
- Explain precisely the reason for the conversation.
- Don't take their lack of outward warmth personally. That's simply their style.
- Become comfortable with their long pauses. They need to think carefully before they speak.
- Take the lead in the interaction.
- Don't schmooze them or try to win them over with flattery.
- Keep the conversation logical.
- Discuss pros and cons of every situation.
- When directing them, go out of your way to give as many details as possible. Outline your desired outcomes as specifically as possible.

Strategies for Keeping the Peace

In addition to the previous interaction strategies, you can also do a number of things to help people (especially those who have very different behavioral tendencies) foster stronger relationships. Doing so will help people work better together, reach consensus more often, and keep the business strong and profitable.

Assign People to Team Projects:

Rather than have family business members work independently on projects, structure the project so that teams can work on it together. Assign parts of the project to those people who would naturally excel at the given task. For example, if the task is to set up the training and orientation program for a new employee, have the Driver set the training session's goals. Have the Impeller lead the orientation/training session. Ask the Stabilizer to create the agenda items and coordinate the logistics at the location for the training session. And have the Careful One create the detailed agenda and gather any extra materials. With each person doing what he or she does best, your group will foster success and build a foundation of working effectively together.

Have Troubled Pairs Lunch Together Regularly:

If two or more people are constantly at odds with each other, have them lunch together or do some sort of other out-of-work activity together. Before sending them out, outline their goals for building the relationship foundation. Give them conversation topics to discuss that are non-confrontational in nature. This will help them find the common ground, establish the relationship upon it, and then build the communication in the future months.

Bring in an Outside Board of Advisors to Add Objectivity:

Sometimes a decision can be so monumental and disagreements between people can be so heated that no family member can help resolve them objectively. That's when you may want to consider bringing your outside board of directors or advisors into the decision making process. These people, who do not work in the business or have any ties to the family, can offer an unbiased view of the situation as well as objective points for consideration. An outside board of advisors often enables family members to view a situation from a different perspective.

Bring in a Family Business Expert:

A family business expert is different than a board of advisors, as the expert/consultant is one person who digs deep into the family issues. The family business expert assesses family business members and guides them through conflicts or to help meet goals. A board of advisors on the other hand will help the family through conflicts or decision-making and business guidance. A family business expert helps families see their challenges in a new light. Consultants often have families complete exercises together so everyone can learn how to better cope and communicate. They also spend a great deal of time getting to the core issues a family is facing and then help develop strategies to overcome the issues.

When All Else Fails

Despite all the strategies and knowledge, challenges between family business members are still likely to occur. That's because families who work and live together will always have an increased comfort level around each other and will be likely to say or do things they wouldn't in a traditional work environment. For this reason, family businesses need to establish strong guidelines that help them run the business like a business. When such guidelines are in place, family members have fewer items to get into disagreements about.

These guidelines include:

- *Having a Clear Organizational Structure:* Everyone in the family business needs to know the company's hierarchy. Just because one sibling is the oldest doesn't necessarily mean that the other siblings report to him or her. The organizational structure will help keep family emotions and childhood roles from dictating how work flows.

- *Creating Accurate Job Descriptions:* In a family business, it's normal for people to take on many roles. When too many people do the same thing, though, they can step on each other's toes and cause conflict. In order to avoid having multiple people working on the same aspect of a project, or to keep one aspect of the business from being ignored, make sure each person has a clear job description of what he or she should be doing. Update the job descriptions regularly as people's duties change.

- *Setting Accountability Standards:* One of the best ways to ensure that all family members in your business are productive and forthcoming is to instill a sense of accountability in each business member. Without proper accountability, family members can go in their own direction, with their own agendas, resulting in tremendous trouble for a family and the organization. Imagine how upset you'd be if you found out that a fellow family business member who had access to the bank account spent thousands of dollars on "business expenses" to decorate his or her office. Without accountability, people often feel they can do whatever they want just because "I'm a family member." In order to maintain the best efficiency and continuity for the organization, the family business members must adhere to strict structure and goals. So, your accountability can be as simple as a strong organizational structure or as professional as an outside board of advisors. Without accountability, you are only as strong as your weakest link.

- *Establishing Performance Review Guidelines:* It's common for family business members to neglect doing yearly performance reviews on each other. Or, if they do them at all, they could be based on familial roles rather than actual work performance. For example, Dad may review his youngest daughter more leniently because she's "always been the baby" (or is a more sensitive Stabilizer), while he reviews the eldest daughter more sternly because she's "the responsible one" (or is a headstrong Driver). Since it's often difficult for family members to conduct performance reviews of each other, consider hiring an outsider to do the reviews. Or, ask a business coach to conduct a 360-degree analysis[1] to get a more objective view of each person up for review. With specific guidelines for conducting performance reviews, you remove any bias and make the reviews objective and based on work performance only.

- *Initiating Sound Compensation and Benefit Rules:* Some family businesses inadvertently pay incoming family members based on their age or status in the family. In other words, an older sibling may earn more than a younger sibling even though the younger sibling is doing more intensive work. To prevent this from occurring, create and initiate sound compensation rules that detail hourly rate structures, salaried pay guidelines, pay increase policies, benefits, and bonus and commission structures.

Communication and Beyond

Communication strategies, combined with sound business practices, will always yield the best results. Do your best to communicate and work with your family members, not against them, to ensure the family stays strong and the business continually grows. Only then will you and your family reap all the rewards a family business has to offer.

Action Item

1. Identify the two people you get along with least. Individually, take each person out to lunch. In order to communicate effectively with the person, go to the lunch date with this chapter's strategies in mind. Use this time to find some common ground on which to start a productive relationship.

2. If a lunch meeting seems like too much too soon, casually share this book with the people who challenge you the most. Ask them to read it, and then make an appointment with them to discuss the book and how you both can use the tools and strategies given to work better together and to communicate more effectively.

Endnotes

[1] This is an assessment that measures how others perceive the family member's performance. It involves a survey of colleagues, subordinates, customers, etc., thus giving the measured individual a 360-degree look at him or herself.

Chapter Six

The Value and Richness in Diversity ~
How to Appreciate Your Fellow Family Business Member

In the previous chapters, we highlighted how the differences we each possess can be a huge advantage when determining who should handle what in the organization or when working through family affairs. When we call on the people who possess the needed attribute for the project at hand, we gain greater efficiency, which results in a higher quality end product.

It's interesting that we sometimes view the differences in behavior and communication as being a problem. The fact is that differences in behavior are not wrong, nor are they bad; they are merely differences. We each possess a vast amount of experience and know-how that adds something valuable to the team. And while we are each different, it's those differences that enhance the family and the business and that actually make the organization stronger. That's why when you develop a strong team or even a strong family, you need a combination of the four behavioral styles to ensure all the work gets done. The goal is to capitalize on each person's strengths to make the business run smoothly.

If everyone in the family business were a Driver, for example, the company would have lots of long-range goals and a lot of head butting, but no one would want to carry out the tasks. If everyone in the family business were an Impeller, the company would be so focused on the customers and the internal relationships that production would suffer or product quality may deteriorate. If everyone were a Stabilizer, the company would have a logical system for day-to-day operations, but would never evolve or take risks that would help the company grow. If everyone were a Careful One, the company would have the most up-to-date research at all times, but no one would take the information to the next level and use it for company growth. This is precisely why we need all behavioral types to run a successful company.

The Behavioral Process Analysis

As you interact with your family members, both at work and at home, you will likely notice various behaviors they each exhibit that rub you the wrong way. Before you let their inherent behaviors annoy or frustrate you, practice the following behavioral process analysis. It will help you see the value of each behavioral type.

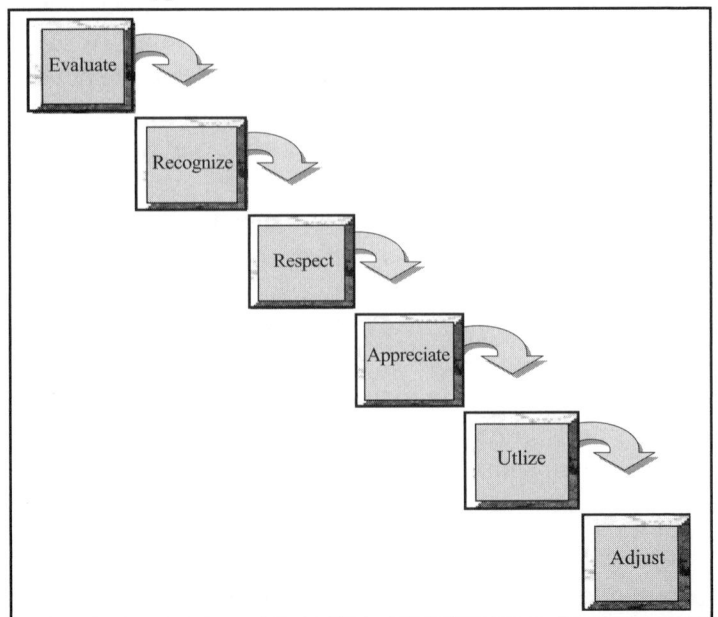

Evaluate

Recognize

Respect

Appreciate

Utlize

Adjust

1. **Evaluate** – Step one is when you evaluate and determine which behavioral tendencies your fellow family business members exhibit. The goal is not to make judgments either positively or negatively *about the person,* but merely to pinpoint the specific behaviors you notice. You can then determine if the person most often fits the category of Driver, Impeller, Stabilizer, or Careful One. Even better is to have each person in your family business read this book, or the very least, do the assessment in chapter three.

2. **Recognize** – Step two is when you acknowledge the differences you notice. Then, when the other person does something you normally find annoying, you can say to yourself, "I won't get upset. I realize that's just the way he or she is."

3. **Respect** – Step three is often one of the most difficult steps. This is when you see past the differences and notice the strengths and talents others bring to the mix, even though you may not initially view them as strengths. For example, if your brother is a Careful One and you are a Driver, you can now view his need for more information as a good way to reduce risk that you may be exposing the business to.

4. **Appreciate** – Step four is when you seek out the other person's viewpoint and ways of doing business to ensure all the business's needs get met. You are able to combine everyone's talents to create a well-oiled business machine.

5. **Utilize** – Step five is an extension of appreciate. This is when you're able to see the other person's strengths and talents as assets to the business. You recognize how the other behaviors positively impact the company's bottom line, and you are eager to take advantage of what everyone offers.

6. **Adjust** – This final step is when you're able to adjust your own behavior to more effectively interact with the other person. You're aware of your own strengths, weaknesses, and talents, and you adjust your approach for each person you interact with. You're able to find some common ground on which to relate, or you meet the other person in the middle to ensure the tasks get done.

Being able to adjust is truly the heart of interacting with others. If we merely identify other people's behavioral tendencies but do nothing to account for those behaviors during an interaction, then the whole identification process was for naught. Our communications will continue to be strained, and true relationships will never form.

Here's how the "adjusting" process would play out in a business setting. If your sister reported to you and was an Impeller, for example, and you had an issue to discuss with her, you may approach the conversation as follows: "You have been doing a great job and people enjoy working on this project with you. I did notice, however, that (address the issue). I know this is something you will understand needs to be fixed and that when you do, people will work even harder and more cohesively with you."

On the other hand, if you were to approach the same situation with a Careful One, you may want to say, "The facts you have been providing have been extremely helpful and appreciated. We did notice (address issue). Would you mind reworking this report/chart/graph/etc. to better explain your points? Your detail is always a benefit when we try to figure out direction."

Notice the key differences in dealing with the Impeller and the Careful One. Since the Impeller is people and relationship oriented, the approach with her needs to focus on the impact her resolved issue will have on others. In the case of the Careful One, where the person is reserved and task oriented, the recommended approach complements her work and also takes advantage of addressing things from a task basis.

Also realize that when you're giving direction to a Driver, the direction needs to be bottom-line oriented and big picture focused. Don't focus on the details. To a Stabilizer, however, you will want to give as much supporting detail as possible and then back away, allowing the person to digest the information for him or herself. The more you adjust your approach based on the person you're interacting with, the more harmonious and productive the encounter will be.

Understanding Behavior for Productive Workdays

When you are able to complete this behavioral process analysis with every family business member, you gain a fresh outlook towards people. Behaviors that once annoyed or frustrated you now have a new, understandable meaning behind them. People whom you once avoided because you simply "couldn't communicate with them" now become your allies. Situations that you hated because you had to interact with "difficult" people, such as in family business meetings, now have a beneficial purpose that you see positively guiding the company.

Even better, when everyone in the family business is aware of the different behavioral tendencies, the company as a whole works harmoniously. Meetings are productive, office relations are less stressful, goals get met, and the company experiences growth. People who once couldn't work together now understand each other and are able to cooperate on projects, with each person contributing his or her strengths to the overall goal.

But you shouldn't reserve this process only for the workplace. You can use this tool with family members who aren't in the business, as well as with friends and non-family co-workers. Whether you're engaging in a formal interaction or an informal one, you can effectively work with each behavioral type and adjust your own behavior accordingly.

A Look Beyond

As you embark on the path to better family business communications, realize that for some families, the teachings in this book won't be enough. Some businesses and families have such deep-rooted communications issues that they need more advanced help. For those families, I would recommend that they bring in experts, such as family business consultants, industrial psychologists, or management consultants who understand family business. Other useful approaches are to attend family business communication seminars and seek out university family business centers, as these resources can help shed light on your family's communications challenges as well as on many other challenges your family business may be experiencing.

Equally important is to always remember that a book, seminar, or consulting session is not a one-time, quick fix to problems that may have been festering for years. Successful communication is an evolutionary process that will get better the more you practice and devote time to it. Those families that have great communication work at it daily. As such, you may want to pull this book out every six months and review it with your family members as a "refresher" course in communications strategies. As your family's communications improve, you can add more and different team and relationship building tools to the mix to enhance the family and the business.

A Family Business is the Best Business of All

Working in a family business gives you many advantages that you couldn't get working anywhere else. Most family business members cite that they receive enhanced professional growth opportunities, added credibility within the community, and increased skill knowledge – all while working with the ones they love. It's a win/win situation that they wouldn't trade for the world.

Yet, in the end, we all know that working in a family business can be both a blessing *and* a challenge. But when you master and understand behavioral and communication styles, you can minimize the challenges and magnify the joys. It's then that you'll experience all the rewards of working in a family business, and you can rest assured knowing that your business is the best business of all.

For more family business communication strategies,

sign up for Laura Michaud's newsletter at www.FamilyBusinessSuccess.net

Need a Thorough Assessment? Contact Laura Michaud for information on a variety of assement tools. Not only will they aid in your communication, but they will also offer support to many other activities, such as team building, hiring, career counseling and management training.

Through Laura Michaud you can receive computerized assessments that go into specific detail on each person. The reports reveal specifics on topics such as:

- The person's general characteristics
- What motivates the person
- How the person deals with conflict and improvement strategies
- How the person is as a manager and what he or she can improve or watch for
- How the person is as a salesperson and how he or she can improve
- What to do if you are managing the person
- What environment the person prefers to be in and works best in

    And more…

Seminars and Keynotes offered by Laura Michaud

- **Who Gets Papa's Chair:**
  Succession Planning – Create a personalized written succession plan on the spot using an eight-step process in this session. Available as a half-day or full day workshop.

- **From the Kitchen Table to the Conference Table: Family Business Communication** – Learn your behavioral style and that of others. Gain useful tools guaranteed to help you communicate better. Available as a keynote or workshop.

- **How To Sell Your Business for Maximum Profit** – Learn how to sell your family business and avoid the mistakes others have made. You will learn the Do's and Don'ts from someone who's done it. Available as keynote or workshop.

- **Inherit the Success not the Stress** – Master up to thirteen business and personal techniques to create balance in a family business member's life. Available as a keynote or workshop.

- **Turn the Tables on Employee Turnover** – Get your managers to become better leaders and get more production from their employees. Available as a keynote or workshop.

- **Increase sales:**
  Creating True Customer Loyalty – Master up to fifteen techniques on how to get close to your customers and create true rapport with them. Available as a keynote or workshop.

Get the Entire Family Involved
Toll-Free: 1-866-372-2636
secured online ordering
www.cameopublications.com

	From The Kitchen Table To The Conference Table: *Family Business Communication* Laura Michaud Paperback (ISBN 0-9744149-4-8): **$17.95**	# Items	Amount
Shipping: USA: $4.95 for first item; add $2.00 for each additional book SC residents please include 5% sales tax.			
	Order Total		

Please Print

Name: _____
Company: _____
Address: _____
City: _____ State: _____ Zip: _____
Phone: (____) _____

Cameo Publications, LLC
PO Box 8006
Hilton Head Island, SC 29938

Sorry no CODs
credit card # _____ expires _____
please sign _____